"Welcome to California, Ava."

My roommate is standing over me, a tray in her hands. The sentence on her T-shirt is unreadable and I freeze on it for a moment, my eyes still half-closed. It's no use, I'm still too sleepy.

"But..."

I sink back into my pillow, but Julia pats me on the head.

"Come on, get up, sleepyhead. I brought you some breakfast. You're not going to let it get cold, are you?"

Okay, it's because there's a delicious smell of coffee that I agree - almost with dignity - to look up at her. I squint again, trying to make my roommate a little less blurry.

"You really can't see without your glasses, can you?"

I fumble with my hand, looking for my glasses. Julia finally helps me find them.

"Thank you."

Once I put my glasses on my nose, the world around me takes shape again. Julia, with her messy hair and mischievous smile, comes into focus. She hands me the tray, topped with buttered toast and a steaming mug.

"Better?" she asks, her eyes sparkling with mischief.

"Much better," I reply, sitting up in bed.

The smell of coffee envelops me, waking me from sleep for good.

Julia sits cross-legged at the other end of the mattress, a satisfied smile lighting up her face. She's always had this gift for taking care of others, even when they don't ask for it.

"So, are you ready for the big day?"

I nod, although the truth is, I'm far from ready.

Today is the first sewing club meeting of the year. The idea of meeting new people, even if they have the same interests as me, makes my stomach turn.

"This is going to be a great year, Ava. We're going to do amazing projects, and who knows, maybe the drama club will finally want our costumes."

I smile, more out of politeness than conviction. The people at the drama club have always looked down on us, as if our sewing skills are inferior to theirs.

"We just need an opportunity to show them what we're made of," continues Julia, full of optimism.

"Yeah, maybe."

But in the back of my mind, I know it's going to take more than just an opportunity to change the way these people see us. Especially me, whose only real concern is the score I can get on my online chess game, or video games, in general. I think I can easily spend an entire night wrapped up in a cozy blanket, watching TV shows, anime and, of course, playing video games. I'm not really a party girl, it's the kind of event that makes me anxious and bored at the same time. I'm not into that at all.

Julia looks at me, a worried crease between her eyebrows. She knows I have trouble mixing with others, preferring the solitude of my room, where I can lose myself in my activities without being judged.

"Hey, the fact that you prefer your quiet evenings doesn't make you a loser, Ava. OK?"

"How did you know that...?"

8

Unexpected

Partners

Our books are also available in e-book.

Find our catalog on:
https://cherry-publishing.com/en/

RILEY S. COLLINS

UNEXPECTED PARTNERS

Cherry
Publishing

That I'm thinking about it...

"I know you too well," she smiles. "Come on, swallow your coffee and get ready! We've got our work cut out for us."

I head for the bathroom and enter the preparation phase. First, I take a good shower, then I brush my hair, which is behaving indomitably. At times, I despair at the sight of my enormous mane of red hair. I look like the Disney princess from the movie 'Brave'. Sometimes people compare me to her. It's great. I'm being compared to the messiest princess in the whole Disney-verse! I try not to be too offended by it and, anyway, my hair has a purpose: to hide me from the gaze of others. When I feel out of place, I can easily hide behind it.

After finally taming my fiery hair into a high ponytail, I choose a comfortable yet elegant outfit: dark blue skinny jeans and a loose cream-colored sweater, with a simple, understated necklace. I take one last look in the mirror, adjusting my glasses. No make-up, just me, natural.

That's how I prefer myself.

"Ready?" calls Julia from our bedroom door.

"Ready," I confirm, taking a deep breath.

We leave our room and walk through the bustling corridors of the student residence. The Californian sun floods the campus with its brilliant light, making the leaves of the palm trees sparkle as they sway gently in the gentle breeze. The air is charged with an invigorating energy, a mixture of excitement and freedom typical of university life. I love it here! Sierra Vista University is the dream life! That is, if you keep away from everyone who's 'cool'.

On our way to the sewing club building, we pass groups of students laughing and chatting, some wearing varsity jackets, others heading for the library, books in hand. The campus is a patchwork of life and diversity. The most magnificent thing is the mountains in the background. It's incredible here, and yet

I have my backpack pressed firmly against my chest, as if I'm trying to protect myself from the happiness I feel.

"Pffiouh, I'm a bit stressed," I confess.

"Everything's going to be fine," retorts Julia as we pass the cafeteria, where the tantalizing smell of lunch is beginning to make itself known.

Students hurry to get their lunch, while others soak up the sun on the lawns, some spread out on towels, others play Frisbee or simply relax between classes.

"It's not easy. We're going to be the losers of the university again. You know that, don't you?"

Julia looks up, as if I've just said something outrageous.

"Who cares? I know 36 different varieties of coffee and I have an uncommon sense of smell, and you, I see you slaughtering frustrated players all night long on your computer. You've got a great level, girl! And let's not even talk about sewing."

It's at times like these, when I receive a compliment, that I feel like hiding a little. I tuck the bottom of my face into my sweater, to conceal myself.

Then, we pass through a small park lined with flowering trees and benches occupied by students with their laptops or books. Birdsong mingles with the distant hum of traffic, creating a soothing melody.

Finally, we arrive at the sewing club, a little way off the main campus roads. The building is old, but charming, with windows overlooking a small garden. The interior is warm and inviting, and the walls are decorated with the creations of members past and present.

We push open the door, and I feel a mixture of nervousness and excitement. This is where I belong, among fabrics, threads, and needles. This is where I feel like myself - and in front of my keyboard - far from judgments and expectations.

Julia nudges me and smiles. It's time to start a new year, to create, to explore and perhaps, to change other people's perceptions.

Don't get carried away, Ava. One step at a time, huh?

As we enter, I immediately notice a few familiar faces and some new ones. The club is an eclectic mix of students, all united by their love of sewing and design.

Among them is Grace. There she is, concentrating on a dress pattern spread out in front of her. Grace is a bit like me, a nerd at heart. She always has headphones around her neck, probably ready to dive into her playlist of video game or anime music whenever the opportunity arises. Her chestnut hair is often tied back in a sloppy bun, and her eyes, behind thin glasses, betray intense concentration. We often bump into each other, sharing knowing glances at nerdy references that only the two of us seem to understand, but never really talking in depth.

Next to her, there are two other members I recognize: Mark, a senior always dressed in elegant, patterned shirts and known for his incredible embroidery talent, and Emily, a freshman, whose creations are always bold and colorful, reflecting her bubbly personality.

I approach shyly, my sewing bag clutched close to me. Julia gives me an encouraging pat on the shoulder before heading towards a group near the sewing machines.

"Hi, Grace," I whisper, not wanting to interrupt her concentration.

She looks up, a shy smile lighting up her face.

"Hi, Ava," she replies, her eyes shining with a recognizable gleam of nerd camaraderie.

I have to admit, it's nice here. There's no need to be accountable because it's just us. It's as if we are alone in the world. Introverts, unable to conform to university society, es-

11

caping into the same passion to forget that outside this place, we're losers.

But let's be clear, we're all champions in our own way! I have a great Elo[1] in chess, Julia is a real nostril on legs, able to smell everything. Mark is an amazing software engineer, Grace is like me - that is, she's very good at competitive games - and finally, Emily is an incredible dancer - when she's not too shy to show it. Because that's the root of the problem, in the end, we're all competent somewhere, but we don't dare show it. Anyway, I'm not looking for fame or cameras. My social networks are all follower profiles. In other words, I don't publish anything, or almost nothing, and I don't have a profile photo. I'm a shadow. A ghost among ghosts. A sort of... inconsistent ectoplasm, wandering from classroom to classroom, hiding behind my hair. The only time I really live again is when I get here. And it's here, too, that I regain a semblance of self-confidence and really dare to talk to people.

Let's face it: we're a nerdy club and nobody really cares about us. I mean... sewing, seriously? Of course we're laughed at. Anyway, it's all about the hockey team and the drama club, with all the prettiest girls on campus and the muscular hunks who act out scenes with them.

Here, at least, I can state my dream loud and clear.

"I want to be a stylist!"

Grace removes an earphone from her ear, then turns to me.

"Did you say something?"

"No, no, nothing..."

No one else picked up on it. When I say, 'loud and clear', I mean 'quietly and discreetly, but at least I say it anyway'.

Sometimes, I dream that I am in big, beautiful fashion shows and imagine the most famous actors of my generation

---

1 The Elo rating is used to rank chess players. The ranking starts at 1000 points and goes up to around 2850 for the best player on the planet today, Magnus Carlsen.

wearing the clothes I design. I want to make them even more magnificent than they already are. I guess I've kind of given up on my own 'makeover'. So, if I can't help myself, I might as well make the others beautiful. I think it's a worthy goal!

I set my things on a free table and take out the sewing pattern I've prepared. It's for a kind of hat I want to send to my family in Michigan, a much colder state than sunny California. I've chosen a soft navy-blue fabric, I hope they'll like it.

As I apply myself to cutting the fabric according to the pattern, I sense a presence behind me. I turn to see Mark, who is examining my work with a benevolent smile.

"This hat looks great, Ava! But you know, it could look even better with some embroidery," he suggests gently.

"Really? You think so?" I ask, a little uncertain.

"Absolutely," replies Mark, pulling a small box of colored threads out of his bag. "Let me show you."

Together, we set to work. Mark patiently guides me, teaching me some simple but effective embroidery techniques. Under his guidance, I begin to add small snowflakes decorations on either side. Each stitch seems to add a little more character and personality to the work.

And while I'm embroidering, of course, Julia is waving at me, trying to distract me. But most of the time, she just gives me the thumbs-up, as if to say I'm doing great. That's what I love most about this club: the friendliness.

After a few hours, the hat is finished. It's beautiful, with its delicate pattern giving it a personal touch. I can't help but smile, proud of what I've achieved.

"Thanks, Mark. I never would have thought of adding patterns like that. They'll love it! Well, especially Tyler."

Mark smiles back, clearly pleased to have helped me.

"You've got talent, Ava. And I'm sure your little brother will be very happy."

I nod, my eyes fixed on my creation. This small victory, however minor, gives me a glimpse of what my life as a designer could be like. A world where I could turn ideas into reality, where I could express my creativity and individuality through clothes and accessories.

I put the hat back in my bag, promising to send it to my family as soon as possible. I'm sure they'll be surprised and pleased to get something handmade, especially from California. It's not like I give out much news, to be honest. The only time I do is when I'm playing online with Tyler. We're on voice chat and he takes the opportunity to ask me how my life is going here. I think my family has gotten used to the idea that I'm some kind of savage who's incapable of opening up to the world around her, and who'd much rather have an evening of video games and TV shows than go out drinking with friends. At first, I honestly thought it would reassure them, but my mother even begged me to go out and have a good time at student parties. My parents even told me that they met at a college party. That day, I cut the conversation short, because I really didn't want to hear any more. At any moment, my mother could nonchalantly announce that it was also on campus that I was conceived, and... no... I don't want to know the details!

"Well," says Julia, standing up and slapping her thighs. "It's about time, isn't it?"

All eyes are on her.

Oh, no, not that, Julia, please...

"We're going to have to choose the president of this club. And that's normal, isn't it? All university clubs have one. I mean, someone has to represent it."

I see exactly where she's going with this, and I don't agree with it at all. I can feel it coming down on me.

My friend glances in my direction and I just try to hide - behind my mane, as usual.

14

"No, no, no, you're not backing out of this, Ava! Come on, on your feet! I'd like to call for a show of hands."

I stand up, a little uncomfortable, as all eyes turn to me. Julia gently pushes me forward, and I find myself facing all the club members. I'm so shy that I don't even dare look them in the eye.

"Uh, I don't think that's a good idea," I stammer.

But Julia, with her usual enthusiasm, leaves me no choice.

"Come on, it's time to vote for our president! Who's for Ava?"

She raises her hand first.

One by one, hands go up in the room. Grace, Mark, Emily. I'm stunned. Me, president? The idea seems so unreal.

"Congratulations, Ava! You're officially the president of the sewing club," Julia announces with a big smile.

Anyway, it's not like there were several candidates...

I feel both honored and terrified. I, who have always preferred to stay in the background, now find myself propelled to the head of the club. I cast an uncertain glance around me, but everyone responds with encouraging smiles.

Well, I suppose it won't make much difference, as long as... nobody ever notices us anyway. It's not like it's going to give me any real responsibility. In terms of decisions, or even budgets. As for the money we have, it's simple: we don't have any. It seems that the university management has forgotten us along the way. It's great that we have this place to meet! We each put in our own money to keep this club going, and for my part, I have to work to earn the precious dollars I invest in the raw materials I sew. Oh, it's not a very tiring job, but let's just say it takes up a lot of my time. As a self-respecting nerd, I spend time on Twitch and Discord. And I get paid for some of my streams on these platforms.

"Thank you," I murmur, still in shock. "I'll do my best."

Mark approaches and puts a comforting hand on my shoulder.

"You're going to be great, Ava. You've got ambition and real talent. We're all behind you," he reassures me.

It's crazy, he is always so kind!

I breathe deeply, ready to take on this new challenge. As president of the sewing club, I'm going to add my personal touch and help each member to flourish in his or her passion. After all, it's in the small steps that big dreams begin to take shape.

"Well, then, it's official," I declare. "I... I guess..."

And then, suddenly, there's a knock on the door. This is extremely odd. Usually, no one comes in except the members already in front of me.

Without waiting for our reply, a man in his forties enters our club. He's tall, with an athletic build and short-cropped graying hair. His piercing blue eyes quickly scan the room before settling on me. He's wearing a university hockey team tracksuit, emblazoned with the Sierra Vista logo. He looks like a man used to authority, and his sudden entrance captures everyone's attention. My heart is pounding. Is he... lost? Why would someone from the university's most fashionable club come to visit us losers?

"Are you the sewing club?"

His voice is firm, almost intimidating. We nod in unison, a little taken aback by this unexpected intrusion.

"All right, then. Who's the president? I need to speak to him or her. Immediately. In my office," he announces.

His gaze finally settles on me.

Oh, no, no, no... That's not possible...

Julia pats me on the back. The traitor! I've only been elected for five minutes. Please, don't make me follow this guy...

"It's... it's me. Ava Crawford," I articulate hesitantly.

16

He stares at me for a moment. His blue eyes seem to be probing me and I hate that. He used to be a soldier. It can't be any other way. He exudes such authority, for God's sake.

"Then follow me. We have things to discuss. It's important," he declares, before turning to leave the room.

I cast a puzzled glance at my friends at the club, who respond with shrugs and uncertain smiles. Mark gives me a sign of encouragement.

"Good luck, Ava. You can do it," he whispers.

With a mixture of nervousness and curiosity, I follow the coach through the campus corridors. His pace is brisk, almost military, and I have to try hard to keep up. I wonder what the coach of the famous hockey team could possibly want to tell me. Is this a collaboration between our clubs? An opportunity for the sewing club to get noticed? Or something completely different? I'm at a loss. Mostly, I feel like I'm following a teacher who's about to give me the lecture of the century.

As we approach his office, my heart is pounding. Whatever the reason for this meeting, it's a crucial moment, not only for me as the new president, but also for the future of our club.

If he wants to talk about sewing, of course...

We arrive at the door.

"I need you and it's urgent. Please, come in."

Let's sum up what I know about the university hockey team: not much. All I know is that they don't even notice us. To them, it's as if we don't exist. We're just uninteresting nerds.

Intimidated, I sit down opposite the coach, as he invites me to do so.

His office is just what you'd expect from a top-level sports coach. Spacious and well lit, it boasts a large window offering an unobstructed view of the ice rink. The walls are adorned with framed photos of the team in action, shiny trophies, and various recognitions. On one side, a large whiteboard is covered with game strategies and formations.

His imposing, solid-wood desk is strewn with files, newspaper clippings and a few personal mementos, like a family photo and an autographed hockey puck. And of course, there's an old military plaque. Ah, I guessed it!

In any case, it has nothing to do with our own club, and I know where the university funding goes!

"I'm Coach Harrison. I have something important to discuss with you," he begins. "To be honest, I only learned of your existence today."

A little too much honesty for my taste.

"I... How can I help you?" I venture weakly, trying to steady myself in my seat.

"We have a problem."

19

Behind him, I can see the athletes training. Just seeing them like that makes me tense. I hate these muscle-mountain types who spend their lives in weight rooms or on sports fields. They've got nothing in their heads. They're just clods who think they're kings of the world when they walk around campus. And, if I don't like them so much, it's also because girls like me are prime targets for these idiots. They seem to make it their mission to harass anyone who doesn't look like them. Most of the time, these guys get scholarships thanks to their athletic abilities, and let's face it: they don't give much of themselves in other subjects. There's only one thing on their minds: hockey.

And when I see them, in the back, in their outfits, laughing and shoving pucks at each other, I shudder.

How awful...

"If... if I can help you solve it, then..."

Come on, be more assertive, Ava!

"We've got a big game coming up," he continues, "and unfortunately our uniforms have been damaged. We need the sewing club to repair them. Ordering new shirts would take too long, and the game is coming up. Plus, it would break our budget."

Oh well...

I'm surprised. I didn't think we'd be called in. Not in any way. I mean... we're pretty invisible.

Suddenly, the office door swings open. It's River Ashton, captain of the hockey team. My heart stops beating for a moment.

River Ashton is the stereotype of the charismatic, popular varsity athlete - basically, everything I hate. He's tall, athletic and, above all, handsome, and he always has that smug look on his face, as if he's entitled to everything. I know his curly, slightly tousled brown hair by heart. It gives him a casual look, but I'm sure that this idiot spends hours in front of the mirror to give himself that unkempt look. And then there are his eyes... blue, sparkling, twinkling with life and making me want to lose myself in them.

Pull yourself together, Ava.

He exudes an energy and confidence that immediately grabs your attention. His smile is far too charming to be real. It's no longer teeth, at this point, but white shields perfectly aligned as if going to war.

"Coach, I..."

"River, damn it, I told you to knock on the... Well, what do you want?"

The sportsman fixes his gaze on me and stares for a few moments, before flashing me a wry smile. Almost immediately afterwards, he turns his head towards his coach.

"Who is this?"

"The savior who's sure to get us out of all the trouble you've gotten us into."

"It wasn't me!" he defends himself. "It was that idiot, Peter."

"Yeah, yeah, save it for the official version. We'll talk about it later anyway. I'm kind of busy right now."

Without another word, River leaves the room, leaving only his intoxicating perfume in his wake.

I REALLY need to get my act together.

As the captain closes the door, the coach sighs.

"A little problem with authority, sir?"

"No comment, miss. Are you going to help us?"

I remain silent for a moment, weighing up the pros and cons.

Despite my reluctance to help those I've always considered adversaries in my university life, the possibility of doing something good for the sewing club makes me hesitate. It's a big responsibility and I've been president for at least... a good five minutes. But I can see myself in my younger days, dealing with those jock jerks. They were always there, pulling my hair, calling me carrot, throwing balloons in my face, and had been for years and years. Things haven't changed that much after all. So, yes, I've had jocks ask me out, and while I admit that physically they don't leave me indifferent, they're so stupid that you could put seeds on a bench, and they'd start pecking at them.

"I... I don't know, Coach Harrison. My club and I... we're not really used to this kind of thing, and besides, I'm not sure everyone appreciates the idea of helping the hockey team," I admit sincerely.

The coach nods. He seems to understand my reservations.

"You're honest. I like that. I understand your hesitation, Ava. But let me tell you this: if you agree to help us, I'll make sure you're properly rewarded. I'm talking about funding for your club, visibility on campus, and official recognition from the hockey team. This could be a great opportunity for you."

His words resonate with me. It's true, this could be a chance for the sewing club to come out of the shadows and earn the respect it deserves. And then there's the idea of bringing our own creative touch to something as prestigious as the hockey team, even though I've never sought glory.

"Besides, it would be a good thing for you and River to work together. It might knock some sense into that idiot."

I nod gently. I understand his arguments, but I don't like them at all. Besides, there's always a dark side to this story: how did they manage to ruin all their jerseys at the same time?

"Can I ask you a question?"

"Permission granted."

He's definitely a military man.

"What happened to your uniforms?"

The coach looks annoyed.

"Well... Peter, one of the guys who plays for us, but is mostly on the bench, left the equipment room door open. So, someone took the opportunity to... um... trash all the jerseys."

I tilt my head to one side. I don't want to be too forward, but... I want the truth.

"I overheard your conversation, you know. River said it wasn't his fault when you accused him."

The coach rolls his eyes.

"You don't need to know any more."

"In that case, you don't need me."

He looks increasingly annoyed. I can see him clutching the end of his desk with one hand, like a pair of pliers.

"For a shy little girl, I think you're very curious."

He sighs and seems resigned when I say nothing more.

"Okay, so it's River's fault. He left the door open while he was having sex in the showers."

Oh, damn it!

"Don't repeat that to anyone. Have I made myself clear?"

"I promise."

"So... Do we have a deal?"

I nod.

"As far as I'm concerned, I agree to help you. But... I still need to talk to the other members of my club."

Coach Harrison smiles appreciatively.

"That's all I ask. Thank you, Ava. You won't regret this. I'll talk to the administration to arrange the details of funding and recognition. You'll have my full support. Talk to the others! But it's urgent..."

I get up, with a big weight on my shoulders. It's a great responsibility, but also an incredible opportunity for the sewing club.

I leave the office to return to the club.

Come on, take a deep breath.

I'm torn between excitement and terror. Coach Harrison's offer is tempting, but I know that not everyone in the club feels an immeasurable love for the hockey team. I open the door to our building and all the members turn to me, waiting for news.

"So, how did it go?" asks Julia.

She looks worried and curious at the same time.

"Well, uh... let's just say..."

I scratch my head, wondering where to start. My friends cross their arms around their chests, some even tap their feet against the floor. They're waiting. Becoming president of the sewing club is definitely no picnic.

I settle down at a table, aware that all eyes are on me, scrutinizing every detail, every expression.

"Coach Harrison has made us a deal," I explain. "He wants our sewing club to repair the hockey team's uniforms, which were damaged in an... incident."

Murmurs run through the room. Grace raises an eyebrow, clearly skeptical.

"And why would we agree to do that? We're talking about the hockey team, Ava! These guys are... rahhhh..."

I take a deep breath.

"There are benefits. Funding for the club, visibility on campus, official recognition from the hockey team. It's an opportunity for us to come out of the shadows."

Julia nods, apparently convinced, but others seem less enthusiastic.

"And in exchange, we become what? Their dry-cleaning service?" criticizes Mark, a worried crease marking his forehead.

"Yeah, well, why would we want to come out of the shadows?" adds Grace. "Every time we try to show off a little, we get shot down like a bunch of losers. It's just not fair!"

"Don't worry. We can show them our talent and our worth.

24

We're not just a sewing club. We're artists, creators, and we're entitled to our share of recognition," I argue.

They still don't seem convinced. So, Julia takes the floor.

"Come on, folks! We're pirates, aren't we? For once, we could be in the light! Besides, we're not the ones who'll be dealing directly with the team, are we?"

This time, my friend turns to me, waiting for my answer.

"Uh... no, no, of course. I'll take care of it myself."

"Did you see him?" she asks with a mischievous smile.

"What are you talking about?"

"You should say 'who' not 'what'," laughs Grace.

I suddenly realize she's talking about River Ashton, and blush. But I don't want to show anything, so I pretend I don't understand. I've only told Julia about this crush, and Grace heard what I was saying that day. I didn't think it would backfire, and besides, they can make fun of themselves! I don't know a single girl at this university who hasn't fantasized about him.

"Come on, come on, don't be shy," Julia teases me. "It starts with a 'Ri' and ends with a 'Ver'. Doesn't that mean anything to you?"

"River? The captain of the hockey team? No, I... I don't know what you're talking about," I say, trying to keep calm despite my hot cheeks.

Julia leans toward me, her mischievous smile still in place.

"Come on, baby, admit it. It's not every day you get to rub shoulders with the star of the campus," she teases. "Lucky you! Ohhh, River... I'm going to fix your uniform..."

"Stop it, I'm not interested in that kind of... distraction!" I reply firmly, although my heart beats a little faster at the mere thought of River.

Grace intervenes, raising her hand to bring the conversation back on more neutral ground.

"We need to make a decision about the hockey team. All those in favor of Ava managing this project with them, raise your hand."

Hands go up slowly but surely. I look around, realizing that the decision has been made: I'll be the one working with the athletes. Great... Part of me is excited by the challenge, another terrified by the prospect of having to work closely with River and his team. I'm literally a basic nerd. A Pokémon not even evolved! I could be eaten alive. But the mere prospect of being confronted with him in intimate situations... I hardly dare think about it.

I've got to let go of all ambiguous thoughts!

"Well, that's decided then. I'll take care of it," I say, summoning up all my courage.

Julia stands up and puts a reassuring hand on my shoulder.

"You're gonna be great, Ava. And who knows? Maybe you'll discover that not all hockey players are brainless brutes."

I smile weakly, hoping she's right. But deep down, I know that this project is much more than just a collaboration. It's a chance to prove our worth and show that the sewing club has a place on this campus. I'm not doing it for myself. Well, not just for me...

But deep down, I'm apprehensive. Those stupid jocks might give me a hard time.

In the evening, back in my room after classes, I'm back to being the person I'm supposed to be: a nerd. No more, no less. Julia isn't here. She's out with the other club members and I've decided to crack open a can of Monster and play video games, while hanging out on Discord. I like it, because it lets me talk to Maeline466, an online friend, between two gaming sessions.

I open the conversation, my keyboard clicking under my fingers.

⋆ **DarkAngelOfDeath666:** *Hey, are you there? Crazy day today.*

⋆ **Maeline466:** *Always here to listen to your adventures. What's been going on?*

I take a sip of Monster, trying to sum up this unlikely day. I really need to talk to an outsider right now.

⋆ **DarkAngelOfDeath666:** *You're not going to believe this. I was elected president of the sewing club, and now I have to work with the hockey team. You know those guys who think they're in a perfume ad.*

⋆ **Maeline466:** *Lol, seriously? You and sports are like oil and water. And those hockey players aren't your kind of guys, are they?*

I smile. I suspected that Maeline would not fail to tease me gently.

⋆ **DarkAngelOfDeath666:** *Exactly. But there's a positive thing. If we succeed, we get funding and recognition for the club. It's an incredible opportunity.*

⋆ **Maeline466:** *Sounds almost too good to be true. Are you sure it's not a trap? And the hockey players... they'll give you a hard time.*

⋆ **DarkAngelOfDeath666:** *That's what I'm afraid of. But I can't let this chance go by for the club. Besides, you know me, I don't give in.*

⋆ **DarkAngelOfDeath666:** *Sure. You'll show them what a real nerd can do. And who knows, maybe you'll come across a cute jock who's not as dumb as the others.*

I blush slightly at the thought, though I refuse to admit it.

⋆ **DarkAngelOfDeath666:** *Don't kid yourself. For me, it's just a job. It's nothing more than that.*
⋆ **Maeline466:** *I believe you... kind of* ;)

Me too, to tell you the truth. I half-believe myself and hope that doesn't do me any harm.

"Hey, Ava! Avaaaaaaaa..."

Julia's voice echoes in the room. I have a splitting headache and wake up groaning.

"Mmmh..."

"You fell asleep at your keyboard. And... you sent 'zzzz' about a million times in a conversation with... Maeline466?"

I blink. Oh, shit... It's 9 o'clock in the morning... What happened?!

I quickly open my e-mail and discover a message from Coach Harrison, telling me that I have an appointment with him this morning at... 9 o'clock!

OH SHIT!

I jump out of my chair and a feeling of panic comes over me.

"Julia, why didn't you wake me earlier? I'm super late for my appointment with Coach Harrison!"

She looks at me, her eyes wide.

"I just got here. I spent the night in another room if you know what I mean. I thought you were just taking a morning nap on your keyboard," she laughs.

I rush to get ready, hastily grabbing my things while brushing my hair. I don't even have time to pick up on the juicy information Julia has just given me about her love life, about which I know nothing. Fortunately, I had prepared my outfit the day before. While I get dressed, I wonder how I'm going to manage this situation.

"Ava, wait, you need something to eat," Julia insists, handing me a cereal bar.

"No time," I say, grabbing the bar and stuffing it into my bag. "Thanks, I owe you one!"

I run out of the room, trying to memorize in my head what I'm going to say to Coach Harrison to apologize for my tardiness. My heart is racing, not only because of the run I'm doing on campus, but also because of the apprehension of this meeting.

Arriving in front of Coach Harrison's office, I catch my breath and knock on the door, a little disconcerted. I glance at my phone: it's 9:19. I'm about to have my head ripped off. The first appointment is really important, from what I could read in the e-mail. It is about setting up the mission and I look like a slob. Well, my clothes are still okay. On the other hand, my hair is a mess, my breath smells like dead fish and I smell like shit because of my geeky night in. I haven't even had time to shower! It's a real shame... I hope River won't be there...

"Enter."

I open the door, immediately apologizing.

"Coach Harrison, I'm really sorry for being late. I had a little hiccup this morning," I articulate quickly.

He looks at me without a smile on his face. He's mad at me. It's loud and clear.

"It's all right, Ava," he grumbles. "Sit down, we have a lot to discuss about the collaboration between our clubs."

I comply, worried about the turn of events. I don't like cold anger in general. If he's mad at me, I'd rather he told me right away. Right now, it's like walking on ice.

The meeting begins, and I focus on the details, determined to make this collaboration a success, not only to prove my worth, but also that of the entire couture club. And to appease the coach, too. Nobody wants to have an ex-military man on their back.

"How did your club take it? Do you have an answer for me?"

"We accept."

"Wonderful!"

He claps his hands, then straightens up to face the window. From there, he seems to observe his players in minute detail.

"You see all these idiots? They need taming!"

"Uh... Okay..."

Is he counting on me to do this?

"Which means you're going to have to be fierce if you want them to cooperate. It's a job between you and me, but also between you and them. If they're behaving like idiots, then you're going to have to get tough."

He doesn't see me, but I nod. I don't really understand what he's getting at. Or maybe I do, but I'm a bit scared: he's trying to point out that I might be in trouble with them. They're always as difficult as they are temperamental. From what I understand, sportsmen are not only stalkers, they're also real divas.

"I hope you've got a bit of temper," he says, turning back to me.

"Ah? Uh... yes, of... of course."

The pout he makes clearly means 'I don't believe you, kid-do'. But hey, at least he's not spitting it in my face.

"If you're not a bit temperamental, believe me, these guys will eat you up. You're a lamb to them, and they're all wolves. We'll try to match your schedule to River's."

Am I dreaming, or is the coach really pulling out River's schedule? Is he in charge?! Is he a... coach or an agent?

Coach Harrison quickly flips through a full planner, mumbling comments to himself. I remain silent, absorbed by the idea of having to deal directly with River. Just the thought of working with him sends shivers down my spine.

"There you go," says the coach, handing me the planner. "River is free this afternoon. This would be the ideal time to meet you and discuss the repairs."

My cheeks flush slightly at the mention of his name, but I do my best to keep calm.

"This afternoon? But I've got chemistry," I protest.

The coach stares at me with a look that leaves no room for negotiation.

"Ava, this is a priority. You have to be flexible if you want this project to succeed. Besides, a missed class can be made up for, not an opportunity like this."

You can tell he's not pro-study.

I weigh my options for a moment before sighing. He's right, this is an opportunity the club shouldn't miss. I have the feeling that meeting River is even more difficult than seeing a shooting star.

"Okay, I'll skip my chemistry class. I'll see River this afternoon," I concede.

"Perfect," he agrees with a satisfied smile. "Make sure you lay out the terms of our agreement and don't be afraid to be firm. River can be... a little difficult sometimes, but he's smart... Sometimes... He'll understand the importance of this project."

I nod, although the idea of having to be 'firm' with River seems a little daunting.

"I'll do my best, I assure you."

After leaving Coach Harrison's office, I head for my classes with a strange feeling in my stomach. The prospect of meeting River this afternoon occupies all my thoughts. I try to concentrate on the lessons, but my thoughts inevitably drift to the afternoon ahead and also to the fact that I'm going to have to shower before I meet him. Otherwise, I'll be REALLY embarrassed.

In literature class, I find myself staring distractedly at the blackboard, the teacher's words seeming to float around me without really anchoring themselves. Julia, sitting next to me, nudges me.

"Hey, Ava, are you with us? You look like you're daydreaming," she whispers to me.

I flinch slightly, then offer her a contrite smile.

"Sorry, I just... I've got a lot on my mind for this afternoon," I admit half-heartedly.

Julia nods, a mischievous smile forming on her lips.

"Could it have something to do with a certain hockey captain?"

I blush, cursing myself inwardly for my obvious reaction.

"It's not what you think," I protest weakly. "It's just... it's a big responsibility, and I want it to go well."

Julia gives me an encouraging smile.

"You'll do great, Ava. You're the president of the sewing club, after all. Show them what you can do. Just don't fall into River's arms, eh?"

"Why, you want him for yourself?"

She giggles and, of course, the teacher notices. We're usually so discreet... That's what the idea of hanging out with the hockey club does to me!

The rest of the morning passes in a blur. My thoughts are constantly turning to the afternoon. When the lunch bell finally rings, I feel both relieved and nervous.

Sitting at a table in the cafeteria, I play distractedly with my food, mentally replaying everything I need to say to River. Julia tries to entertain me with jokes and anecdotes, but I'm barely paying attention.

And then there are the jocks in the corner of the cafeteria, laughing at us. I don't even feel like raising my voice. I prefer to hide behind my mane.

"Don't listen to them," says my friend. "They're stupid."

"And we're going to work for them."

"With them," she corrects me.

Yeah. That's what she says...

The hour approaches inexorably. When it's time to leave for the appointment, I stand up, a lump of anxiety in my stomach.

"Are you going to go now?" asks Julia, seeing my serious expression.

"Yes, it's time," I say, trying to sound confident.

She gives me a high-five, as if that's going to help.

Well, that helps a little. I feel more confident.

I head for the building housing the hockey team's rink, my heart beating wildly. As I approach, I hear the familiar sounds of a game in progress: the squeak of skates on the ice, the cheers of spectators, and the clash of sticks against pucks. There aren't many people in the stands, but it's still noisy. Especially the girls in the corner. They can't stop shouting at the players - especially River.

I roll my eyes. What a bunch of scatterbrains...

I stop for a moment at the entrance, observing the game. My eyes are immediately drawn to River, who stands out not only for his impressive physique, but also for his ease and leadership on the ice. He moves with an agility and confidence that confirms his reputation as the team's star. Classy...

Come down to earth, Ava...

As I approach, River picks up the puck, performs a series of deft maneuvers and, with astonishing precision, sends the puck into the opposing goal. A thunderous round of applause and screams erupts from the stands, where the girls are still raving about his performance.

A bunch of groupies...

I suddenly feel very small and intimidated. River lifts his mask, revealing a triumphant smile. His eyes briefly scan the crowd, bathed in admiration and approval. Then, with relaxed assurance, he leaves the ice, to the congratulations of his teammates.

I take a deep breath to gather my courage. It's my turn to talk to him, to approach him as president of the sewing club. I walk towards the players' exit, mentally preparing myself for the interaction, while he claps hands with his friends.

River, still surrounded by his teammates, notices my presence. His blue eyes settle on me, a hint of curiosity in his gaze.

"Uh, River? I'm Ava, from the sewing club. We have an appointment to discuss uniforms," I say, my voice betraying my nervousness.

Just as he's about to answer, a girl passes me.

She's tall, with blonde hair cascading over her shoulders. Her bearing is confident, almost arrogant. She approaches River with a familiarity that clearly indicates they know each other well. I immediately understand that this is Bethany, River's ex, whom I've heard so much about. When the two of them got together, it was like a reality show. It was all the campus talked about for months. The most famous cheerleader and the hottest jock in college. Together. Just like that. They were the perfect combo, but a few weeks ago, it all fell apart for some reason.

"River, baby!" she says in a honeyed voice, placing a hand on his muscular arm. "You were incredible on the ice, as always."

River offers a polite smile, but I notice a slight tension in his shoulders. He seems less at ease than usual.

"Hi, Bethany. Thanks," he replies briefly.

She moves even closer, lowering her voice so that only the

two of them can hear. She's not even paying attention to me, who's... literally right in front them. Have I mistakenly worn my invisibility cloak? Am I some kind of female Harry Potter? If so, I wish someone had warned me.

"River, you know, I often think about us... what we had. We should try again, don't you think?" she insists.

I feel uncomfortable, an unwitting witness to this intimate conversation. River, however, remains calm and shows no sign of approval.

"It's over. I'm focused on hockey right now," he replies firmly. "I don't have time for anything else."

The answer doesn't seem to please her and the beautiful blonde raises her voice a little.

"Say you're busy banging hookers in the locker room, yeah!"

"Give me a break. You don't know what I'm going through, so just leave me alone, okay?"

I feel a shiver of respect for him. He's handling the situation with a maturity I wouldn't have suspected.

Bethany sighs, disappointed, then turns to me, staring critically. She chews her gum. There's all the disdain in the world in her eyes as she looks at me.

"And who are you?" she asks, one eyebrow raised.

"Uh... Ava, from the sewing club. We have a joint project with the team," I explain, trying not to show my confusion. "It's... it's Coach Harrison who..."

"It's okay, I don't need your life story, honey."

"Uh, er..."

"Is that all you know how to say?" she continues.

That's why I hate jocks and cheerleaders. All they're good for is harassing other people and putting them through painful schooling. Do they ever make it in the real world? No, they don't! Most of the time, they're failures of the worst kind. It's unbearable. I really don't want to get into it with her. I don't think she's worth it anyway.

If Julia only knew what I was going through. Getting close to these people is like sticking your hand in a snake's nest. Well dressed, good-looking snakes, but snakes, nonetheless. And in this case, the snake doesn't hesitate to bite!

"OK, big glasses, since you don't seem to be very brave and, on top of that, you're mute, I'll leave you to it."

She goes her own way, leaving me speechless. I hate being the one who gets stepped on like that. If we'd been in a video game, it would have been so different! I'd have chewed her up, that pretentious little bitch. But this is the real world, and I do have big glasses. There's not much I can say in my defense, and as the bitch leaves me alone, I turn to River, who's already talking to his teammates, promising to go for a drink with them right now.

Oh, boy, I've got to be firm. That's what the coach said!

I approach him with determination, to put Coach Harrison's advice into practice.

"River, we need to talk about collaboration between our clubs," I say, in a voice more confident than I feel.

He turns to me, an amused smile on his lips.

"Oh, that's right, it's now. Guys, I'll join you in a few minutes," he announces to his teammates before turning completely to me. "So, what do you want to talk about, uh... Lara?"

"Ava."

"Ah, yes, that's it..."

His proximity and charisma intimidate me, but I try to stay focused.

"We need to plan uniform repairs, and it's important that we start as soon as possible," I mumble, trying not to show how much he's affecting me.

River smiles again, as if reveling in my embarrassment.

"All right, let's plan it. But you know, I think you could speak a little louder. Even at two centimeters from you, I can't hear anything."

To mark the occasion, he moves closer and my cheeks flush.

"Well, I'm able to speak... louder, yes."

"Great. And are you sure you have enough 'grip', for this kind of work? These uniforms are a real mess."

His eyes roam over my face, as if they're scrutinizing me.

Is he hitting on me openly? It's... so strange. This has never happened to me before.

I don't feel particularly comfortable. I feel like prey.

"Don't worry about that. I can be very serious when I need to be," I reply, trying to hide my confusion.

River laughs softly, leaning in a little closer.

"I don't doubt it, *Lara*. But you know, I'm not as bad as everyone thinks. You'll see, working with me can be quite pleasant."

His proximity makes my heart beat faster. It's disturbing how charming and disconcerting he can be at the same time.

He's deliberately getting my first name wrong. He wants to confuse me, and the worst part is, it works.

"I'm... I'm here to work, River. Nothing more," I retort, trying to maintain a certain professional distance.

He raises his hands in surrender, a smirk on his face.

"As you wish."

"How... how do we proceed?"

"You're the expert, aren't you? I'm just the jock, after all."

The one with nothing on his mind.

"Won't the jerseys you have here do?"

"These rags? No, certainly not for the important game we're playing, and they're not flocked. Follow me, please. We're going to the locker room."

Locker room?...

I suddenly feel nervous about entering the hockey team's locker room, a place that seems to be a sanctuary for them. River leads me through the corridors, his confident, relaxed gait in stark contrast to my own unease. I need to take a deep breath. Come on. It's no big deal, after all. It's just a locker room. It's just where they shower and change. *Naked.* A place I'm normally totally forbidden from...

We arrive at the changing rooms, and River opens the door with an ease that indicates he's in his element. The interior is spacious, with lockers lining the walls and benches in the center.

"Here they are," he says, pointing to an open locker where several obviously damaged jerseys are stacked.

I approach to examine them. Sharp cuts and tears are visible on the fabric. This is going to be quite delicate work. It's obvious that we'll have to be meticulous and skillful. And these are clearly deliberate snags. Whoever did this did it with scissors!

"Yes, it's going to be complicated, but nothing's impossible, I..."

Absorbed in my inspection, I'm surprised to turn around and find River shirtless, changing his sweat-soaked jersey. Despite myself, my gaze lingers on his perfectly sculpted torso. His muscles are well-defined, the result of many hours of training and effort. His skin is lightly tanned, and droplets of sweat bead down his pecs. He's undeniably well built, every curve and line of his body seemingly carved from marble. He's either a Greek god or I don't know. Even my virtual crushes, in the games, aren't this well built, it's crazy...

I quickly look away, feeling my cheeks turn a shade of red. The sudden proximity and the sight of River in such a state of exposure make me incredibly aware of our solitude in the dressing room.

Something could be happening right now.

But I've never done anything with anyone.

"Uh, I... I think I can do something about the jerseys," I stammer, trying to refocus on why I'm here.

River gives me an amused smile, clearly aware of the effect he's having on me.

"Perfect, I'll wait and see. And sorry about the view, I didn't mean to make you uncomfortable," he says, pulling on a clean T-shirt.

Oh, of course, you did.

"It's all right," I retort quickly, my voice still betraying my confusion. "I'll draw up a plan and let you know how to proceed with the repairs."

"Great. So, I'm going to join the others. I'll leave you to it. Lock up tight on your way out," he continues, sending me the key ring.

I catch it on the fly, and he leaves without even turning around.

I stand there, a little stunned by this interaction. River Ashton is definitely more complex and intriguing than I could have imagined.

Just as I'm about to take a closer look at the damaged shirts, the locker-room door swings open. Bethany bursts into the room, slamming it shut behind her. She has a wry smile on her face and a defiant gleam in her eyes. I don't like this at all. What does she want from me?

"So that's it, eh? You're playing dressmaker so you can get closer to River and hang around him?" she says acidly.

I look at her surprised and slightly frightened. Bethany approaches me, her heels clicking on the locker-room floor. I feel like I'm trapped. Instinctively, I take a few steps back, but I know I won't get far.

"Listen, Bethany, right? I... I'm not hanging around River.

We just have a common project for the club," I say, trying to remain as calm as possible.

She doesn't seem to be the easy type. Not at all...

"Oh, right! Just a project, eh?" she retorts, widening her smile. "You know, I don't like new girls who try to play in the big leagues."

Before I can react, she gives me a hard shove. I stumble backwards, losing my balance, and end up on the shower floor. Bethany then rushes to the taps and turns the water on full blast.

Cold water immediately drenches me, soaking me from head to toe. I scream, surprised by the sudden icy shower, and Bethany bursts out laughing. She seems to take a malicious pleasure in seeing me soaked and helpless.

"Here's a little lesson for you," she lets out between laughs. "Stay where you are, darling. I think that should cool you down a bit, don't you? I thought your ovaries were going to explode when you stood next to River."

Without another word, she leaves the changing room, leaving me there, completely soaked and humiliated. I stand still for a moment, shocked and frozen, before pulling myself together. Trembling, I turn off the water and try to regain my composure after the violence of what has just happened to me.

I hate jocks and their groupies. They're all the same.

I leave the changing rooms, my heart heavy and my clothes soaked. Every step towards my room is an ordeal, under the curious and sometimes mocking gazes of the students on campus. And then, of course, there are the remarks when I pass. The 'nice wet T-shirt contest' or the 'look at that cunt!'

I feel humiliated, vulnerable, and most of all angry at myself for being so easily tricked by Bethany. Why did she take it out on me for free? I hadn't done anything. I just want to fix the hockey jerseys.

I know I shouldn't react. I shouldn't take it personally. The world is cruel and that's the way it is, but... I can't help it. So, I try to hide behind my red mane.

Finally, I reach my room and quickly lock the door behind me. Alone, in this bubble of safety, I allow myself to drop the wall of strength and confidence I've been trying to maintain. The tears begin to flow, gently at first, then louder and louder, until I'm sobbing openly.

I let myself slide against the door; my arms wrapped around my soaked knees. Each sob takes away a little of the frustration and humiliation I'm feeling. I'm angry at Bethany for her cruelty, at River for his flippancy, and at myself for my naivety. I don't belong here, and I won't make it.

After a few moments, I straighten up with what little dignity I have left, then dry off and change completely, all the while muttering heartfelt insults at that pest Bethany.

"You want to pick on girls who have a little crush or fantasy about your ex, moron? Spoiler alert: you'll have to fight the whole campus! What a bitch, that one..."

After wiping away the last of my tears, I head for my computer. A gaming session seems to be exactly what I need to distract myself from this disastrous day. The virtual world offers an escape, a place where I can lose myself in adventures and challenges that have nothing to do with campus drama. Normally, I'd be in class by now, but never mind. I can't bear the thought of seeing other students right now. It's my social anxiety that's going to be happy: for once, I'm going to listen to it more than I should.

I launch my favorite video game, the screen lights up and transports me to a world where I feel more at ease, far from mocking glances and judgments. Here, I'm not the girl who was humiliated in the locker room, but a competent and respected player. Serves all of them right!

I immerse myself in the game, concentrating on quests and battles. Every action, every victory, gives me a sense of control that reality seems to have taken from me today. In this world, I can be whoever I want to be, without fear of the Bethany's or the River's of real life.

> * **Maeline466:** *Shouldn't you be in class?*
> * **DarkAngelOfDeath666:** *Yeah, I should. But let's just say I've had an... interesting morning. I need a break.*

I immerse myself more deeply in the game, letting myself be absorbed by the missions and battles. Every victory gives me back some of the confidence I've lost in real life.

> * **Maeline466:** *Tell me about it! It's not every day you skip school. That's got to be juicy!*

I sigh, reluctant to share the humiliating details of my morning. But Maeline is a friend, even if we've never met in person. She's always been there for me, through good times and bad.

> * **DarkAngelOfDeath666:** *Let's just say I had an... incident with a cheerleader and got soaked in the hockey club's locker room. Long story. Will this do?*
> * **Maeline466:** *Oh wow, campus drama! Do you want to talk about it?*

I take a second to think. Talking might make me feel better, but at the same time, I don't want to relive that humiliation. Not right now.

> * **DarkAngelOfDeath666:** *Maybe later. For now, I just want*

to smash monsters.

    ★ **Maeline466:** *Okay. Destroy them.*

Like any self-respecting geek, I have several screens on my desk. The first is for gaming, the second for Discord, the third for surfing the web and consulting my social networks. And speaking of which, while I'm waiting for a game to load, I come across my Instagram messages. A notification, to be more precise. What could it be?

Probably more spam.

I open the page and discover, with a touch of dread, that it's... River.

What does he want from me?

4

It's almost 10p.m. Julia isn't here yet. I don't know what she's up to, and I'm sitting like an idiot in front of my computer screen. The game has just started, but I'm still stuck on River's message. But it doesn't say much...

★ **River:** *Hi.*

But it's the simple fact that he's talking to me, damn it!

River Ashton, 13,700 subscribers, a photo of himself scoring a goal in a hockey game, the university's top male prospect, Coach Harrison's star, probably destined for a pro career... And he sends me... 'Hi'. I look like an idiot. I click to follow him...

★ **Ava:** *Hi. How are you?*

My hand trembles slightly as I type the message. Why is he contacting me? And on Instagram no less? It can only mean one thing: he wants to talk about our jersey collaboration. But why now, and why in this way?

★ **River:** *Yes, I'm fine. You weren't easy to find on Insta, you know? Anyway, sorry about this afternoon. I didn't have time to deal with it, but you see, the coach puts a lot of pressure on me, so...*

I almost blush.

I read and reread his message. Is he apologizing? It seems so contrary to the image I have of him.

★ **Ava:** *Don't worry. I understand.*

My answer is brief, my fingers still a little uncertain on the keyboard.

★ **River:** *We'll meet tomorrow, OK? 10 a.m. at the hockey rink if that's okay with you. We'll talk about it a little more calmly.*

Of course it's good for me.

I close the app, a mixture of apprehension and curiosity filling me. River Ashton, the captain of the hockey team, really wants to help me. It's an opportunity, a chance to showcase our club's talent. But at the same time, it means having to work closely with him. And... with Bethany around, I'm not sure I want to.

I dive back into the game, trying to concentrate on the game in hand, but my thoughts inevitably drift to tomorrow's meeting. How will it go? How should I deal with him? Crap! I've just killed my character! I can't stay focused with all this on my mind.

Suddenly, I'm startled. A hand has just grabbed my headset.

"Hello, Earth to Ava, this is your roommate who just got home and wonders why you weren't in class today, damn it!"

"Huh? Ah! I..."

"You've got a phone, sweetheart, it's not just for taking pictures. You can also... I don't know, mmmh... pick up?"

"Sorry, Julia."

She sits on her bed, glaring at me.

"And then, with the noise your headset was making, I thought we were being attacked by the army. So, what happened? What should we do about the club? We're all waiting for your instructions now. You're the one in contact with River."

I suddenly feel overwhelmed by the weight of the day's events. Words are hard to come by, but I know I must explain to Julia what has happened.

"Julia, I'm so sorry. I've had a... complicated, really complicated day," I begin, my voice trembling.

She sits down next to me, worried.

"Ava, what's wrong? You're not the type to skip class for no reason."

I take a deep breath, trying to gather my thoughts.

"First of all, the interview with Coach Harrison this morning... it went well. We've got a deal. I told him that the sewing club has agreed to repair the team's jerseys. And then there was... that incident with Bethany."

I pause, feeling the tears threaten to fall.

"She... she humiliated me, Julia. In the locker room. She pushed me into the shower and soaked me. Everyone saw me come dripping back onto campus. It was horrible."

I can see the anger and concern in Julia's eyes.

"That bitch! She had no right to do that to you. Are you all right?"

I nod, trying to be stronger than I feel.

"It's okay... it's okay. But that's not all. River contacted me on Instagram. He wants to meet tomorrow at 10a.m. to talk about jerseys. He seems to want to help. That's... that's pretty cool, isn't it?"

Julia frowns, visibly surprised.

"River contacted you? On Instagram? That's... unusual."

"Yes, I was surprised too. But I think it's a good thing for the project. I... I just have to make sure everything runs smoothly. I'll keep the club informed."

My voice is uncertain, betraying my anxiety for the meeting ahead.

"If she comes after you again..."

"What will you do, eh?" I ask, shrugging my shoulders. She's silent.

"Girls like us stay in a corner and keep our mouths shut," I conclude. "We're not the... the popular ones who... who can fight or compete with the ones that everyone likes and who... who get likes on social media. You know what I mean? We... we're the invisible ones."

My throat clenches just saying it, but it's the truth.

"Hey... we're not losers, okay?"

"So, what are we, Julia? Hmm? When was the last time you had a boyfriend? When was the last time you went to a party?"

She stammers out a few unintelligible words.

"Don't talk to me about last night. I know you weren't getting laid," I continue. "You were probably with Grace, crocheting. Am I right?"

Julia looks down.

"That's what I thought."

"We were crocheting, but we were having a rom-com movie marathon, so..."

"It's worse! Face it."

I take my headset out of her hand and screw it on my ears.

Shit! We're at the bottom of the food chain. If she hasn't figured that out by now, there's nothing more I can do for her.

I fall asleep around 3 a.m., full of bitterness. I know I shouldn't have spoken to Julia like that. That she was just trying to help me. But I couldn't help myself. I'm exhausted by our condition. We're all failures on this campus. No more, no less. This is not the life I want to lead. Far from it.

★ ★ ★

It's 7:30 when I wake up. No steaming coffee above me this morning. I get it. I really wasn't nice yesterday. I was so frustrated and angry about what had just happened that I forgot my usual delicacy.

Julia is already getting ready. She doesn't even glance at me.

"Julia, I..."

"Don't say anything. Don't say a word. I know."

"Please don't be like that."

"And how, then? You're saying I'm invisible! That might be OK for you, but not for me. Me, I... Sometimes, I want to be seen, OK? I'd like to be noticed too. That's why I try to make an effort."

I know you do...

"Look, I'm sorry. I didn't mean to hurt you by saying that. I'm just afraid we're... we're making a fool of ourselves. Can you understand that?"

She sighs, then sits down on my bed.

"Because we're 'not girls like that'?"

"Yeah. Exactly," I retort. "And I don't know if I want to try to become one. I mean... what do hip girls look like? Bethany?"

"They look like girls who don't say 'hip'."

I pout because she's got a point, then get up to start preparing for my turn. It's a very meticulous choreography. Every bit of our tiny room serves a purpose. So, to avoid stepping on each other's toes, we've organized ourselves: each has her own shower time, her own place to drink coffee, her own corner of the room to dry her hair...

"You don't have that problem," adds Julia, straightening up in turn.

"What do you mean?" I ask.

"You don't realize how lucky you are. You're finally going to be seen."

"Are you talking about these meetings with River? I'm telling you; you don't want to be me…"

Julia stops dead in her tracks, then looks at me as if I've just said something outrageous.

"You don't know how much I'd kill to be in your shoes!"

I'm surprised by the intensity of her reaction. Julia, usually so calm and composed, expresses a burning desire to be recognized, to be 'seen', as she puts it. It makes me wonder. Maybe we're not so different after all. We both have our insecurities and hidden desires. I want to hide behind my hair forever, and she wants to hide behind a confident façade.

"Julia, I don't know if being 'seen' by these people is really a good thing," I retort as I finish getting ready. Especially if it means having to interact with people like Bethany and River. They're… horrible. I'd much rather be playing video games, I guarantee it."

"But this is an opportunity to change things. To show what we're really worth. You have this chance. You've got to seize it," she insists. "Do it for the losers that we are, okay?"

I nod. I understand her point of view, but I don't share her enthusiasm at all.

"I'll give it a try. Shall we?"

We leave the room, walking side by side to our morning class. The tension of the previous day seems to have dissipated, replaced by a kind of mutual understanding. Julia is my real best friend, after all. Yes, real, as opposed to Maeline666 who is my virtual best friend. The distinction is very important.

This morning's class is biology. The teacher is passionate about his subject, but I struggle to concentrate. My thoughts keep turning to the meeting with River. I'm putting too much pressure on myself about all this.

How will it go? What will he say? How should I behave?
I look at my phone discreetly. No message from him. What did I expect? That we'd suddenly become best friends and he'd start texting me on Instagram? It's dumb, and I'm way too naive.

Julia, beside me, is diligently taking notes, glancing at me with concern from time to time. She knows I haven't followed anything yet. But she also understands.

When the bell rings, I get up, feeling a little lighter. I'm going to see him again and I don't know why, but... I really like the idea. That is, if we forget that Bethany is liable to come down on me at any moment.

"I'll see you after your date with River, okay?" Julia hugs me before leaving.

I laugh at her remark.

"It's not a date! It's a business meeting!"

"Ah, and don't forget to tell us about the club. We need to know a bit in advance, anyway!"

"Okay," I reply, a shy smile on my lips.

Let's head for the hockey rink, where I still don't know what sauce I'm going to be eaten with...

I'm already expecting to hear the sound of the sticks again, but nothing. There's only silence and, finally, the whistle of someone skating.

It has to be him.

He's so fast he looks like he's flying across the ice. I spend a few moments contemplating him, before clearing my throat.

River stops, looks at me, then leaves the ice, smiling.

I swallow, suddenly feeling small and insignificant in front of him. River Ashton, the captain of the hockey team, is not only a talented athlete, but also almost intimidatingly handsome. His presence is so strong, so imposing, that it fills the space around him, leaving little room for anyone else.

He takes off his skates and walks towards me. His steps echo on the floor. Each movement is precise and measured, as if he's aware of the effect he's having on those around him. River stops right in front of me, his gaze plunging into mine. A smirk forms on his lips, and he nods in greeting.

"Hi, Ava. Sorry about yesterday, I was in a bit of a hurry," he says in his low, warm voice.

I try to gather my thoughts, aware that I need to be professional and focused on the project. But part of me can't help but be fascinated by this man standing in front of me, a perfect blend of strength, charisma and beauty. I have to pull myself together. He knows he's irresistible and he's playing it up. I'm sure he knows it. He can't just wake up in the morning and say, 'I'm really just a normal person, no big deal.' No. He must devour himself with his own eyes! There's no other way.

"No... no worries. It's, it's great, Instagram, for talking. It works well. It's a good social network."

Shut the fuck up, Ava.

"Er...? Yeah. Well, we're here to organize the repairs, aren't we?"

Will he try to hit on me again or show me he's too good to be true? The first time, he smirks. The second time, he goes topless. I fear the worst because I have the strange impression that River is making a pass at me. Not that I don't like it, but I'm not used to it, and I have no idea how to react. Besides, I mustn't fall into this kind of game. He's a seducer. A playboy of the worst kind. I'd just be some kind of trophy for him. I'm not even sure if he's doing it consciously, either. He must be so used to people falling for him, he must act like that with everyone.

"Yes, yes, I... I had some ideas, and... you... you must tell me if..."

"Carrot."

"Huh?"

"It suits you, I think."

He looks at my hair mischievously. Not mocking, no. Just mischievous. And it really throws me off.

"What? No, don't..."

"Carrot. Right, Carrot. It's kind of cute, a carrot."

I open my mouth to protest, but no sound comes out. It's as if I've suddenly gone mute.

"Follow my lead. Yesterday, I barely showed you the place, so... we'll take the trouble to make it better."

I follow him, trying to keep calm and concentrate on the project in hand, despite the unexpected nickname he's just given me. 'Carrot,' really? It vaguely reminds me of schoolchildren's taunts, but coming from River, it's both disturbing and curiously amusing.

Once in the changing rooms, the atmosphere changes. The place is both familiar and intimidating, filled with echoes of competitions and victories. Just yesterday, I was under a shower, fully clothed, in this very room. What a bad memory...

River walks down the corridor, shows me the facilities, the different rooms, and finally stops in front of an open locker, where damaged jerseys are stacked. Just like yesterday.

"Right, so... I entrust them to you, or...?"

I approach to examine them again.

OK, maybe Mark will know how to handle it. Besides, Grace is competent too. We should be able to do this.

"It can be done, but it's going to take a lot of time and precision," I explain. "We're going to have to reinforce the damaged areas so that they'll hold during the games. And... make the whole thing harmonious."

River nods, seeming to understand the magnitude of the work involved.

"How long do you think it will take?" he asks.

53

"Uh... a while, though. Several weeks."

"Several weeks...? Holy..."

"What?"

River suddenly looks stressed.

"We've got the big game at the end of the season coming up."

"It's going to take a lot of patience, I'm... I'm sorry."

He nods, then sighs. He looks deeply upset.

"So, uh... do we have to take all this stuff to the sewing club?" I ask.

"Yeah."

I wonder how involved he'll be in repairing jerseys. I don't expect him to sew with us, but will he stick around?"

"Coach wants me to take care of all this with you," he adds, grabbing the pile of jerseys.

Now I'm surprised, but suddenly I have the answer to the question I was asking myself. Why should he do it?

"Can I ask why?"

"To punish me," he replies simply.

He grabs a large duffel bag from a corner, then dumps the whole pile inside.

"Punish you for?"

"You're very curious, Carrot."

"I don't like that nickname at all."

"And what are you going to do to stop me? Cry?"

I frown, looking obviously annoyed.

"Oh, no, you're going to frown? Now that's... wow, way too powerful. That's my weak spot!"

"Stop laughing."

River leans towards me, a mischievous smile on his lips. He's so close that I can feel the warmth of his body and the fresh smell of his cologne. His gaze plunges into mine, and I feel my heart beating faster, as if it's trying to escape my chest.

"Laugh? Me? Never," he replies, laughing softly. "I just think it's cute when you get angry."

I blush, irritated by his ability to throw me off balance. I try to pull myself together, reminding myself that I'm here for the sewing club, not to be distracted by a charming hockey player.

I take a step back and hit the wall behind me.

"Be careful, Carrot, you can't go through walls yet."

"I..."

"You're always leaving pauses in your sentences. So, tell me: are you just insecure, or do you love to be interrupted?"

He destabilizes me so much. I'm not comfortable. I always have this feeling that I could be eaten alive.

"No, I don't like being interrupted."

"So, assert yourself."

"But..."

"See? You're still giving me space here to interrupt you. So, I'll take it."

He puts his arms around me, against the wall.

How did it all go so wrong so quickly?

"And you're trying to hide behind your hair," he says. "Be more assertive, Carrot. You're going to spend time with the hockey team."

He's just inches from me. I can feel his breath. And if my ears were just a little sharper, I'm sure I could even hear his heartbeat through his veins. He's so intimidating...

"Could you..."

"What? Let you go?"

"I..."

"Come on, talk!"

I can feel the frustration rising like a wave.

"Let go of me, you stupid jock!"

It came out on its own and I shake off his hold. He doesn't look pissed, despite what I said. No, it's more like he's...

amused.

"Ah, you're finally waking up. About time you did. So that's what you think? That jocks are big, dumb clods?"

I thought he was a bit different. But I guess not.

"Maybe yes."

"Great. I think geeks like you are stupid too. See, two can play at that game."

"Stupid?"

So, I get offended, then resume:

"Oh, sure, the stupid geek doesn't know anything, while the sportsman knows very well the chemical composition of... beryllium!"

"BeF_2."

I blink.

"What's up, nerd? Should we drop them off at your geek club, or just sit here and talk chemistry?"

"But..."

River straightens up, looking as confident as ever and amused by my reaction.

"Come on, Carrot, we've got work to do. And don't worry, I'm not going to eat you. Not yet, anyway," he says with a wink.

I'm both frustrated and intrigued by his attitude. It's obvious that he likes to play, but I can't help wondering if there's something more behind his charming smile and teasing. River, in spite of everything, seems to have a certain depth that I hadn't anticipated.

"All right, let's go. But no jokes," I warn, moving away from him.

We emerge from the changing rooms, he carries the sports bag heavily laden with damaged jerseys. As we make our way to the sewing club, I try to stay focused on the project, but I can't help casting furtive glances at my comrade. He walks with an ease and confidence that captivates me.

He was able to give me the chemical formula for beryllium... how is that possible? He can't be... a nerd, can he? He can't be captivated by this kind of thing and at the same time display such confidence!

"So, is this it?" he asks, standing in front of the door.

I freeze in front of the sewing club, aware of the impact River's presence might have on the other members. They're not used to seeing people like him, especially not such a popular hockey player on campus. To them, he's a kind of celebrity, an almost mythical figure.

A unicorn... I hadn't thought of that. They're literally going nuts!

"Uh, just a second, River. I'm just going to... check something inside," I say quickly.

I rush in, leaving the champion waiting at the door. My heart is pounding, not only because of River's proximity, but also because I'm about to announce to my geek friends that a hockey star is about to enter our sanctuary.

"Guys, listen up! River Ashton is right outside the door and he's coming over to discuss the jerseys. Please try to stay calm!"

Astonished looks and excited murmurs answer me. Some hardly seem to believe that River Ashton, in the flesh, is about to enter our club. I implore them with my eyes to behave normally.

"Are you serious?" exclaims Grace.

"Do I look good?" asks Mark.

"I don't think you're his type Mark" replies Julia.

"Please don't do anything weird!" I beg them.

I go back to the door, open it and let River in. As soon as he enters, the atmosphere changes. Eyes widen, mouths part, and some members seem to freeze in place. River, on the other hand, flashes a confident smile and greets everyone with a nod.

Oh, boy, are they going to look weird...

"Hi everyone. I'm here for the jersey project," he announces.

The club members look at each other, some blushing, others trying to hide their excitement. An awkward silence settles in. Despite my recommendations, River's presence seems to have a paralyzing effect on them.

I cough slightly to get their attention.

"Uh, so... River's going to help us with the jersey repairs. We're going to start working on them right away," I announce, trying to restore some semblance of normalcy.

River gives me an amused look, as if he knows how much he's disturbing the usual order of things. I blush, realizing that despite my best efforts, the mere fact that he's there turns our sewing club into a theater of silent admiration. I should have known better.

Nobody talks. Nobody moves, and finally it's Julia who jumps into the fray, lifting the shirts to see their condition.

"Ah, yes... It's not going to be easy."

"We're going to have to make several proposals," I announce. "Which means..."

"I have a feeling we'll be seeing a lot of each other," River cuts me off. "That's fine by me, Carrot. I've got to run. I've got class now."

Like he's really going to class, that one. I'm sure, he's going to have sex with a girl and... rah, why am I thinking about this?

"Uh, well... all right. We'll... we'll look into it."

River greets us, then leaves the club. Everyone waits a few moments, just to make sure he can't hear us from the other side of the door, and then their joy erupts:

"Well, that was crazy!" says Grace.

"I think he looked at me," Mark agrees.

"Hey, it's okay, y'all: it's not Kanye West either, all right?

We're... we're just doing our job."

Julia gives me a mocking smile.

"Wow, Miss President is really coming into her own, I see."

"It was always there. I just... needed to realize it."

"We're going to get some coffee," says my friend. "Who wants coffee? "

Inevitably, all hands go up and we leave the club. I understand perfectly well that all this is an excuse for Julia. She's going to be especially indiscreet.

"What the hell was that?!"

She looks overexcited in the corridor leading to the cafeteria.

"What are you talking about?"

"'That we'll be seeing quite a bit of each other,' she laughs, hooking her fingers together. "Seriously?! Wait a minute, this is crazy!"

I'm blushing like crazy.

I bite my lip, feeling a wave of confusion and doubt wash over me. My mind is a whirlwind of questions and uncertainties. Is River really interested in me, or is this just a way for him to have fun? The way he calls me 'Carrot', the way he teases me and gets close to me... it all makes me feel alive, but at the same time, I'm terrified of being wrong about his intentions.

"Ava, are you listening to me?" asks Julia, drawing me out of my thoughts.

"Uh, yes, yes, of course, I was... I was thinking," I stammer.

Julia looks at me with a mischievous smile.

"About River, right? You know, it's normal to wonder. But don't let it go to your head. You'll see how things turn out. He's so... charismatic!"

She has no idea how much.

I nod, trying to mask my nervousness. The idea of working closely with River, of seeing him regularly, makes my heart beat faster. I can't help but wonder if there's even the slightest chance that he's really interested in me. Me, Ava, the slightly shy, awkward geek, up against River Ashton, the confident, charismatic hockey star.

It doesn't make sense.

"You should take advantage of the opportunity. Who knows? Maybe you'll discover another side of River, the one that not everyone sees," suggests Julia, patting me on the shoulder.

Like the side of him who knows the chemical formula for beryllium?

I smile weakly, letting the idea germinate in my mind. Maybe Julia's right. Maybe behind River's charming smile and self-assurance there's something more, something I could discover as we work together.

"On the other hand, I must warn you," she murmurs more seriously.

"What?"

"I ABSOLUTELY want to know EVERYTHING."

But at the same time, a little voice in my head reminds me to be careful. River is popular, surrounded by girls like Bethany, and I don't want to find myself hurt or humiliated again. I need to keep a cool head and focus on the project, without getting distracted by illusions or unfounded hopes.

However, despite all my reservations, I can't help but feel a thrill of excitement at the idea of seeing him again. River Ashton has already begun to occupy an important place in my thoughts, and I'm still not sure whether that's a good thing or a bad thing.

Rather a bad one, I'd say.

"So, are you going to see him again?"

"Well, yeah. I don't have a choice."

"Oh, how happy you must be!"

She really doesn't understand anything. In that respect, I

can't say I'm as enthusiastic as she is. Mostly, I'm afraid I'll end up in a lot of trouble, but I guess time will tell.

What possessed me to accept?

I glance at my watch. It's 5:30 sharp and I have an appointment with River at 6:00. I'm not ready at all. Firstly, when he came to the club yesterday, it caused quite a stir, and secondly, I spent a good part of the night trying to decompress on video games, where I got all the rotten advice from my virtual friend. She advised me not to "trust guys like that!"

Oh, right... like I'm a rabbit and he's a wolf.

Am I?

Suddenly, I'm wondering.

Here I am, in front of my mirror, wondering how I'm supposed to behave. Should I be aloof and professional, or open and friendly? River is a mystery to me, and I'm afraid of making a faux pas. Julia, as enthusiastic as ever, tries to give me some last-minute advice.

"Ava, relax! You're great just the way you are. Don't try to be someone else," she says, adjusting the collar of my T-shirt. "You don't need that, okay?"

I give her a nervous look in the mirror. That's easy for her to say. She doesn't have to deal with the subtle advances-or not-of one of the most coveted guys in college. I haven't really told her that River made a pass at me and... I don't dare. She'd probably think I was imagining things.

"What if I say something stupid? What if he thinks I'm just

another uninteresting geek?" I worry aloud.

"River approached you for the project, not to judge you on your social skills. Besides, I'm sure he finds you interesting; otherwise he wouldn't have bothered sending you a message, would he?"

She's got a point. A small point, but still. It's true that we exchanged on Instagram, and I honestly still can't believe it - it's so crazy.

He didn't follow me, though.

I take a deep breath, trying to calm the butterflies in my stomach. Julia's right. I need to focus on the project and not let my insecurities get the better of me.

Purely professional. Come on.

"OK, let's go. I don't want to be late," I say, grabbing my bag.

"On the other hand, next time you have an appointment..."

"Yes?"

"Try to go to bed early. You look like you've been up all night destroying other players while chugging energy drinks."

Another point for her. That's... totally what I did!

And I'm not ashamed of it!

Julia and I are particularly complimentary because she's a very heavy sleeper and I have the annoying habit of playing online until very late. In that sense, I couldn't have wished for a better roommate.

On the way to the hockey rink, my thoughts become muddled again. River and I come from such different worlds. Him, the sportsman adored by all, and I, the president of a sewing club who prefers to spend her evenings online rather than at parties. How can we work together without it becoming strange? Can this ever become normal?

Just as we arrive, Julia ditches me. I don't have the courage to go alone again - because of Bethany. But now that we're approaching the sound of crosshairs, it's obvious that my friend is fleeing too. She's no more comfortable with these big, muscular, tattooed athletes than I am.

"Are you going to be okay?"

I nod feverishly and Julia gives me a pat on the shoulder before leaving me.

Come on. Come on.

When I arrive, I see him already there, waiting. River is leaning against the wall, immersed in his phone. He raises his head at my approach and greets me with a smile that makes my heart beat even faster. I mustn't let his beautiful eyes fool me. He's a flirt. He's not the right guy for me.

"Hi, Carrot. Ready for our work session?" he exclaims, putting his phone away.

I blush instantly at the nickname, but somehow it makes me smile. There's a familiarity in his voice that puts me slightly at ease.

"Yes, ready. Let's go," I retort with a confidence I don't really feel.

As we head towards the sewing club, I promise myself to keep an open mind. Maybe, against all odds, River and I really could work well together. Maybe this collaboration could be the start of something new for me, something unexpected, but enjoyable. Mmh... No, I think I play too many video games.

But for now, I'm concentrating on his footsteps in front of me, trying not to think too much about what might happen. After all, as Julia said, I just have to be myself. That's all I can do.

I take a deep breath, which River doesn't fail to notice.

"How's it going? You look nervous, Carrot."

There I am, standing in front of the sewing club door, my heart beating wildly.

It's just River, after all. River, who seem to take a malicious pleasure in flirting, but who, deep down, is only in it for the jersey project. That's what I keep telling myself over and over to try and convince myself. Do I mean it? I don't know myself. He seems so convincing when he's openly flirting with me. And then, he stays close to me, gives me teasing looks... I get the impression he's having fun.

I push open the door and enter the club, empty at this hour. The subdued lighting and silence contrast with the usual racket of our work sessions. River follows close behind, his sports bag slung over his shoulder.

"So, we're alone?" he asks, a smirk on his face.

I turn back to him, surprised by his remark.

"Uh, yes, I guess so. The others must be busy," I stammer, aware that his presence here, just with me, could be interpreted in many ways.

He places his bag on one of the tables and stretches, as if to relax. His gesture draws my gaze to him, and I can't help noticing how... good looking he is. I quickly look away, cursing myself inwardly for letting my mind wander.

"I thought we could think of it as a... date," he suddenly drops, staring at me intently.

My heart stops. A date? With River? My thoughts race. I analyze his words, trying to figure out if he's serious or still toying with me.

"A date?" I repeat, my voice betraying my confusion.

I frown to give it away.

"Yes, why not? We're working on a project together, just the two of us, in an empty sewing room. Sounds like a date, doesn't it?"

He looks amused, as if he appreciates my confusion.

I don't know what to say. A part of me is flattered, intrigued, but the other is terrified of trying to decipher his words too much, of deluding myself.

He's fucking with me, it's not possible.

I prefer to reframe the situation right away before he laughs in my face.

"It sounds more like a business meeting," I reply, trying to keep a cool head.

He moves a little closer, reducing the distance between us.

"Rho... A business meeting? Can't we relax a bit, have some fun while we work?"

His tone is light, but his eyes never leave mine.

I feel trapped and my heart is pounding. In a way, the idea is seductive, if true, but I also know I'm walking on dangerous ground. River Ashton isn't just anyone. He's the kind of person who attracts attention, desired by many. And I'm just Ava, the president of the sewing club, who may kick ass at online monsters, but is still a no-name in real life. What am I doing here, even entertaining the idea of a date with him?

"We're here for the jerseys, River. Maybe we should concentrate on that," I manage to articulate in a voice more assured than I feel.

He seems surprised by my reaction, given the look he's giving me.

We have a very specific goal: to define how we're going to repair these damn jerseys. It's not going to be easy. All the seams have to be redone, and in any case, I don't think we'll have enough time to finish for the big game that's coming up. It's mission impossible, and I'm committed to it. I think I'm going to have to beg Julia to pull all-nighters with me... I might as well avoid adding a ridiculous flirtation with River Ashton on top of it all.

"What's wrong, exactly?" he asks suddenly.

My heart beats a little faster and... a little harder.

"Nothing... nothing, why?"

"You're lying. I can tell. I'm having an effect on you, so why are you trying to hide it?"

What a nerve this guy has!

Now I'm really blushing. I don't have any mirrors to look in, and that's just as well, because I think I'd die of shame.

"You're... you're imagining things. For the jerseys, I thought we could..."

Instead of listening to me, River continues to stare at me with an intensity that doesn't displease me. I take a deep breath, mid-sentence, because I feel like he could jump out at me at any moment.

"That we could?" he repeats.

"Ah er... Yes, I..."

"You stopped in the middle of your sentence a good ten seconds ago."

What an idiot! I hate being like this, I feel dumb and I don't like it at all. Come on, I've got to regain some dignity, it's not possible.

"What are you really interested in, hmm?" he asks suddenly. "Are you really passionate about sewing?"

"Oh, uh... pretty much, yeah. I like... I like this, but I like other stuff too, you know?"

"Like what?"

Why is he so insistent? Usually, people just take my brief answers and move on! But not him. River seems picky and the more I talk to him, the more I realize he's smart. Probably more than he lets on, anyway.

"I like traveling, music, watching TV shows, eating healthy food, ..."

"Oh, come on, stop it," he laughs. "A girl like you?"

To ease the discomfort I'm feeling right now, I let my hair slide down in front of part of my face, lowering my eyes.

"Come on, Carrot, get that mane out of your face. I'm sure there's more to you than that. You've just given me a list of passions from a person with no personality whatsoever, and I don't think that's you. I feel there's something else. Something juicier. You're the kind of person who has a hidden vice..."

Like calling myself DarkAngelOfDeath666 online and slaughtering my opponents unscrupulously every night?

That must be what he wants to talk about. It probably is.

"No... I assure you."

"I don't believe you," he retorts, coming dangerously close to me.

Oh, God, he's so close I can smell him. I've never been this close to a boy, it's... it's weird.

I take a step back, my back hitting the table behind me. River doesn't stop, though. He places his hands on either side of me, framing me without touching, but close enough for me to feel the warmth of his body. His gaze plunges into mine, intense and curious.

"So, what's your vice, Carrot? What do you do on the sly when you're alone?" he insists, his voice lower, almost a whisper.

I feel trapped, my heart beating so fast I feel like it could be heard all over the room. On the one hand, I want to tell him, to reveal this part of me that no one else knows - except Julia. On the other, I fear his reaction, the possibility that he'll laugh at me or, worse, not take me seriously. Maybe he'll even have fun telling people on campus. I'm already known as the weird girl, and now I'm going to be branded a big geek!

But he's so fucking handsome. I like him so much... It's indecent! Why is he hitting on me so hard?!

"I... I play online. As DarkAngelOfDeath666," I finally blurt out, my voice trembling with apprehension.

His smile widens, and to my surprise, his eyes shine with genuine interest.

"Really? Yeah. That's pretty cool. What kinds of games?" he

asks, his tone devoid of mockery.

I'm taken aback by his interest. I had imagined all sorts of reactions, except this one.

"Strategy games, mainly. And a few FPS[2]," I retort, feeling a little more at ease.

"I'm impressed, Carrot. I didn't expect this of you, but I'm glad to see you've got some interesting passions," he says, straightening up and releasing me from his grip.

I take a deep breath, relieved by the air flowing freely around me again. River picks up the bag containing the jerseys, ready to continue our collaboration.

"You know, I think we have more in common than you might think. I'd love to talk about it some other time. For now, I guess we'll just have to get on with the jerseys, won't we?"

I nod shyly and we set to work. I can't wait to tell Julia all about it tonight. Or tomorrow. Depending on my emotional state. For now, I'm starting to think, with River, about what the team wants, and shaping my pattern around his demands. It's not going to be easy at all, but at least he's getting his hands dirty.

I measure, cut and sketch out plans for repairs while listening carefully to River's suggestions. He's surprisingly knowledgeable about what his team needs in terms of jersey functionality and style. I'm pleasantly surprised by his involvement and realize that he doesn't take our project or his role as captain lightly. This makes the task less daunting and, in a way, more enjoyable. He's less of a hothead than I thought he'd be. Quite the opposite, in fact, but that raises another question in my mind: what was he doing with a girl like Bethany? Because, in his case, unlike him, she doesn't look like the penguin who glides farthest over the ice floe. She's the very archetype of the stupid, cruel cheerleader, who uses her assets to crush all the

---

2 First Person Shooter.

other girls around her.

"You know, I didn't expect you to know so much about sewing, or at least about what you want for your team," I confess, impressed by his knowledge.

River laughs softly, a sound that stirs something deep inside me.

He's having the craziest effect on me. I don't know whether I want him to kiss me or run away!

Maybe a bit of both...

"Well, I can't sew, but I know what makes us feel good on the ice. Besides, I have to admit I did a bit of research after our first meeting. I wanted to make sure I could contribute properly. And to make up for my mistakes..."

His admission makes me smile. The idea of River doing research to better understand our collaboration touches me. It shows a side of him I hadn't seen before, a willingness to get involved and respect the work of others, even in a field as far removed from his own as sewing.

We work together for quite a while, discussing technical details as well as lighter subjects. From time to time, our eyes meet, and each time I feel a little chill. River seems to prolong these moments on purpose, and I can't help wondering if he feels the same way.

Finally, as the hour draws on, we both realize that night has fallen. He stretches for a long time.

"I suppose I should be going," he says, looking at the time on his phone. "We've come a long way, don't you think?"

"Yes, that's true. Thank you for helping," I reply, sincerely grateful for his support.

He stands up, gathers his things, then stops in front of me, hesitating for a moment.

"Ava, I really enjoyed tonight. It was cool."

His gaze is intense, and I feel nervous again, but in a different way. This time, it's a nervousness tinged with excitement and curiosity about what the future might hold, because a million questions are running through my mind. I wonder what it's like when that happens. Well, it's true. I never have. I mean, I've never... I've never done this before. Spend time with a guy, fall for him...

I'm imagining too many things. I have to stop RIGHT NOW.

"I enjoyed it too," I murmur, unable to hide my smile.

River hands it back to me, then walks away, leaving me alone with my thoughts and a feeling of unexpected contentment. I put the material away, turn off the lights, and close the sewing club door behind me, all the while thinking about this strange but wonderful evening.

River and I may have started this project in different worlds, but something tells me we've just found common ground, and maybe more. He's openly flirting with me. I can't put this down to guesswork anymore. And I want to believe that he's sincere. That this isn't just some stupid dare he's set himself, thinking he can easily 'bang the little geek on duty'. I really hope so... Anyway, I don't know why I'm thinking about this at the moment, since it's all still a blur.

I need a break!

When I get back to my room, I rush to my computer, eager to dive into my online game, but also to reflect on everything that's just happened. It's my way of taking refuge in a world where I feel in control. But tonight, strangely enough, I feel just as in control in reality, thanks to this unexpected partner. It's as if... through this new relationship, he's giving me the self-confidence I need. And that comes from the way he looks at me, interested and approving. It's ridiculous and I feel a bit pathetic to reason like that, but I can't ignore reality: it's how I feel.

I immediately notice a message from Maeline466 flashing

in my inbox. I click on it, eager to share the evening's events with her.

* **DarkAngelOfDeath666:** *Hey, you'll never guess what happened today...*
* **Maeline466:** *Tell me everything! I hope it's juicy!*

I begin to tell her, trying to be vague about my feelings, but detailing how River was actively involved in the project, his research, and his surprisingly insightful suggestions. I also mention, with some reluctance, the moment when he referred to our work as a 'date'.
Maeline reacted immediately.

* **Maeline466:** *A DATE?! With River Ashton? Ava, this is huge! Do you realize?*

I feel myself blushing even though no one can see me.

* **DarkAngelOfDeath666:** *It wasn't really a date. You know how he is... he's always flirting. But yeah, it was... nice.*
* **Maeline466:** *Nice, eh? ;) I told you, be careful with that kind of guy.*
* **DarkAngelOfDeath666:** *I know, I know. But he's different from what I thought. He's really interested in the project, and he... he knows the chemical formula for beryllium, can you believe it?*
* **Maeline466:** *LOL, so that's your criteria now for recognizing that a guy is worth it?*

I smile, enjoying the lightness of our conversation. It's good to talk to Maeline, it brings me back to reality and keeps away the butterflies that seem to have taken up residence in my stomach since that evening.

⋆ **DarkAngelOfDeath666:** *Maybe… Anyway, I'm going to concentrate on the project. That's the most important thing.*

⋆ **Maeline466:** *Well said! Well, show them what you can do, DarkAngel. And if you ever need to let off steam, I'm here for a game.*

I smile, grateful for her support. Maeline has always been a pillar for me in this online world, and it's comforting to know that she's there, no matter what's going on in real life. Since screens have become such an important part of our lives, virtual friendships are bound to follow suit.

⋆ **DarkAngelOfDeath666:** *Thank you, Maeline. I think I'm going to need it.*

I'm getting ready to start a game, but the exhaustion of the day suddenly catches up with me. My eyes half close, and before I know it, I'm falling asleep on my keyboard - yes, again!

Am I some kind of rock star at the sewing club? I think so, yes. When I walk in this morning, everyone's jumping up and down to ask me questions!

I feel overwhelmed by the sudden attention. Every member of the club seems to have a burning question on their lips, all focused on one subject: River. They want to know every detail of our working session, every word exchanged, every look. I wasn't prepared for such curiosity, and it makes me incredibly uncomfortable. They hardly need to look at me for me to immediately understand that they are burning with curiosity.

I try to weave my way through the flood of questions, trying to remain vague and divert the conversation to the project itself, but it's a losing battle. Their interest in the jerseys seems to have waned in favor of their fascination with my budding relationship with River.

What relationship am I talking about? Oh, boy... I'm really imagining things!

"So, what was it like working with him? Is he that charming in person?" asks Grace, her eyes sparkling with excitement.

Even she ended up falling for the jocks!

"He's... professional," I stammer, desperately trying to find a way out of this uncomfortable discussion.

"Oh, come on, Ava, you can tell us more!" insists Mark, a mischievous smile on his lips.

I feel trapped. I have no idea how to manage their curiosity without revealing too many personal details. That's when Julia steps in, her gaze piercing through me as if she could read my mind.

"Let her breathe, all of you!" she exclaims. "Ava will tell you what she wants when she feels ready."

My savior to the rescue!

I give her a grateful look, relieved that she's coming to my defense. Julia, however, doesn't give up so easily. As soon as we're alone again, she watches me with a smile that speaks volumes.

"So, how was it, really? You look... different," she teases.

"Different? What do you mean?" I retort, trying to act as if nothing has happened.

"I don't know... more fulfilled, maybe? It's like something happened between the two of you. You've been flirting, haven't you?"

I blush violently, unable to hide my surprise at her intuition. Julia bursts out laughing, clearly delighted by her discovery. Shit, I've burned myself like a beginner - which I am. And she's taking advantage because she knows it!

"I knew it!" she exclaims. "So, is it true? River Ashton has a thing for our Ava?"

I feel torn between wanting to tell her everything and the fear of appearing naive. In a way, I'm proud of myself, proud to have attracted the attention of someone like River, even if I don't yet know where this will lead. But I have to be discreet about it. Bethany's ghost is still on my mind, and I feel like the walls have ears everywhere. Especially since that bitch probably hangs out in the hallways more than she does in class.

"I... we just worked together."

Julia gives me a friendly nudge, her knowing smile warming my heart a little.

"Of course, you just 'worked' together. And I'm the Tooth Fairy," she scoffs.

I can't help but smile, suddenly feeling less alone with my secret. Maybe sharing this experience with Julia isn't such a bad idea after all. It makes me feel a little more normal, a little more like the other girls who have stories to tell about boys. I feel like I…fit in a bit more? It's weird when you put it like that. I wouldn't like my integration or validation as a person to come through someone else's eyes. It goes against my values. That said, it's not just anyone. It's River…

Deep down, I know that what happened with him wasn't just an ordinary story. Okay, maybe he's an easy flirt, but there was something there. I felt we were on the same wavelength. I can't ignore it.

I feel overwhelmed by their curiosity, my head buzzing with uncertainties and memories of last night. River and I shared a moment of real complicity, far beyond the simple framework of our project. But how can I explain this without revealing too much about myself, without betraying the budding trust between us? And above all, without looking like a girl who gets ideas and shows off?

The day's classes follow one another in a haze of distraction. I can't concentrate, every word the teacher says takes me back to River, his smiles, his looks. And then, in the middle of a particularly boring lesson, my phone discreetly vibrates in my pocket. It's an Instagram message.

It's from River.

My heart misses a beat. I sneak a glance around before discreetly taking the device out of my pocket. The message is simple, but it makes my heart beat even faster.

★ **River:** *Hey, Carrot. Can we get together tonight? I've got something for you. It's a surprise…*

77

Why does he want to see me? What kind of surprise is this? My fingers hesitate on the keyboard, torn between excitement and nervousness.

★ **Ava:** *Why? What kind of surprise?*

His answer is not long in coming, but it doesn't seal my intrigue.

★ **River:** *Ah, if I told you, it wouldn't be a surprise ;) Just trust me on this. And... don't tell anyone, okay?*

I bite my lip, more confused than ever. Keeping this to myself, especially with Julia and the others pressing me with questions, is going to be a real challenge. But something about the way he said, 'Trust me' compels me to agree. Just seeing his profile enter my Instagram DMs is a kind of honor and pride I find hard to hide.

Julia turns to me.

"You're OK?"

I nod, then smile, before picking up my phone again.

★ **Ava:** *Okay. Where and what time?*

I quickly put my phone away, a ball of excitement and anxiety forming in my stomach. The day passes in a blur, my thoughts completely consumed by what awaits me tonight.

Back in the bedroom, I try to immerse myself in my online game to decompress and take my mind off tonight. Maeline466 is there, as always, ready to listen and advise me.

★ **Maeline466:** *So, this hockey star? Are you going to tell me* *what's going on?* ;)

I smile in spite of myself, touched by her interest.

⋆ **DarkAngelOfDeath666:** *He wants to see me tonight. He says he has a surprise for me. But I'm not supposed to tell anyone.*
⋆ **Maeline466:** *Wow, that almost sounds like a date! Be careful, Ava. Guys like him can be tricky. If you're lucky, he'll pull out his d...*
⋆ **DarkAngelOfDeath666:** *Hey! Stop it! Gross!*
⋆ **Maeline466:** *What, you wouldn't like it? If you want, I'll take your place. I've had a look at his photos. Maw-yum, your man!*

OK, that's too much for me, I'd rather like her message and put this conversation on hold for now.

Finally, the exhaustion and emotion of the day catch up with me. My eyes slowly close while I'm still sitting at my keyboard. When I wake up a few hours later, I have the imprint of the keyboard on my cheek and a feeling of panic: it's almost time to meet River.

I really need to stop staying up so late.

Especially since I'm still on the Maeline conversation page and, realistically, I've sent her several hundred "zzzzzzzzzzzzs".

I rush to get ready, my heart pounding at the thought of what awaits me. What's the surprise? Why me? Despite everything, a part of me is excited, curious to discover what River has in store for me.

Here I am, staring at my mirror, trying to decide what to wear. I'm not used to preparing for this kind of thing. River told me it was a surprise, and I have no idea what to expect. My hands shake slightly as I rummage through my wardrobe looking for something that might be appropriate for a date... or whatever it is River has planned. Why, for that matter, does he always have to be so unpredictable? On the other hand, I can't refuse him anything. Every time he looks at me with those big eyes, I feel like I'm going to melt. I don't know what to say. It's as if he has an unbelievable power over me. I shouldn't let him have so much. I should... I should be able to take it back, but I can't. I mean, he only had to offer to see me outside the hours when we're supposed to be repairing the jerseys for me to come running. Why would he do that? I haven't the slightest idea.

In the end, I choose a simple outfit, but one that I think is pretty: jeans that fit me well, a top that's a little more elegant than my usual T-shirts, and a jacket in case it's chilly. I stand in front of the mirror, analyzing my reflection. It's strange to see myself like this, a little more dressed up than usual.

How about a little lipstick?

I borrow some from Julia - who only wears them for special occasions and at the same time, she enters the room and whistles in admiration.

"Wow, you look great! Where are you off to?"

I blush, uncomfortable, but also a little proud that she's noticed my efforts.

"Uh, River asked me to meet him tonight. He said it was a surprise. Sorry, I took your lipstick, but..."

Julia bursts out laughing, clearly amused by my nervousness.

"Oh boy, a date with River Ashton! You have to tell me absolutely everything when you come back. Lipstick's on me! With an opportunity like this, you clearly need it more than I do."

I give her a look that's meant to be disapproving, but deep down I'm glad to have someone to share this moment with. I take a deep breath, grab my bag and head for the door.

"I... I don't know if it's a date," I say, trying to keep a certain composure.

"Go on, have fun, Ava. And relax!" she adds, pushing me gently towards the exit. "Because of course it's a date, you ninny!"

"Hey! Julia! No, don't..."

I leave the room, my heart beating wildly. What does River have in store for me? And why am I both terrified and excited at the idea of spending time with him outside the sewing club? *A date? A real one?*

But is it even a date? Because if he sees that I'm dressed like I'm going out on a date and I'm not, I'm going to look like an idiot.

I don't have enough confidence in myself, I need to pull myself together...

As I walk to our rendezvous, my mind is a whirlwind of questions. River is an enigma to me, and I can't help wondering where this is all going to lead. I feel as if I'm about to plunge into the unknown, not knowing whether I'm going to swim or sink.

He's arranged to meet me in front of the campus, and as I'm getting out, I spot him. He's leaning against his car, waving at me.

As I approach the car, River opens the passenger door for me, a gesture both gallant and a little surprising coming from him. I settle into the seat, a little nervous, but also excited to find out what he has planned for us.

"If DarkAngelOfDeath666 would be so kind..."

I have a feeling he's not going to let that go.

The car is comfortable, and the atmosphere inside is pleasant, with soft music playing in the background. River climbs in on the driver's side and gives me a reassuring smile before starting the car.

"Ready for an adventure?" he asks me, as he pulls the car onto the road.

I nod, curious to know where he's taking me. I feel my heart beating a little faster, torn between apprehension and anticipation. Usually, this kind of thing only happens to other girls. It doesn't happen to me. It's as if, all of a sudden, I've been thrust into someone else's life, and I like it. I didn't know I had a taste for it until I actually tasted it. I always told myself it wasn't in my best interest, but now I think I'm starting to enjoy it. I had convinced myself that I wouldn't enjoy these moments, but I must admit that having an absolute hunk driving next to me is not unpleasant.

As the car pulls away from the campus, I stare out the window, watching the scenery go by. River seems confident behind the wheel, focused on the road while trying to keep the conversation light to put me at ease.

"I hope you like what I've planned," he says after a moment.

I turn to him with a shy smile.

"I'm sure I will," I retort, trying to hide my nervousness.

But he still hasn't clarified things, after all! Is this a date, yes or no?

The journey continues in a pleasant atmosphere, punctuated by laughter and discussions on a variety of subjects. This is a different side of River that I'm discovering, far from hockey and the competitive atmosphere. Here, in the privacy of his car, he's more accessible, more human. He's really not as dumb as the other sportsmen I've heard of and dealt with. Does he give himself an image to please the people who are fans of his? All of a sudden, I get the feeling that River isn't who he says he is and... strangely enough... I like it.

"You seem to have prepared yourself with care," he says. "I didn't try as hard as you did."

Is he kidding? He could put on a garbage bag, and he'd still be more attractive than I am! It's totally unfair!

"This? Oh, no, I... I just put something on real quick, you know, pff! Just chillin'. I'm cool!"

It was the LEAST cool thing in the world to say.

So much so that he starts laughing outright.

"You're hilarious, Carrot. You know that?"

"Ah yes...?"

"Yeah. You're prepared, like for a date. You took it seriously, then."

I shouldn't have?! I knew it!

"Lighten up. You look like you're about to blow a fuse," he laughs. "You're beautiful."

He's just telling me. Like it's nothing. Just a compliment thrown in. For me, it's much more than that. It's totally... new!

Gradually, my nervousness gives way to a feeling of comfort. River has a way of putting me at ease, and I'm really starting to look forward to the rest of the evening.

"So where are we going?"

"In the most beautiful place."

River stops the car in the middle of nature, just a few kilometers from the campus. It's simply beautiful. We light up our phones with flashlights, and I realize that I'm crazy for following a guy all the way out here in these conditions. But River inspires a confidence in me that I can't begin to explain.

"Are we almost there?"

"Almost."

"Because right now, it's the worst date of my life," I tease.

"The worst, but also the best because it's the first, isn't it?"

He can't see me blushing because we're in the dark, but I feel red as a tomato, and the rest of the way I keep quiet.

"Almost there..."

River moves the branches of a bush and... there I am, in

front of a breathtaking sight: a moonlit lake, stretched out and peaceful before us. The mirror-smooth surface of the water perfectly reflects the silvery light. Around the lake, the trees stand like dark silhouettes against the night sky. The air is fresh and filled with the damp scent of earth and water, mingled with the sweeter scent of wildflowers hidden in the darkness. The silence is broken only by the gentle murmur of water and the distant call of a night bird. I feel small in this natural immensity, amazed and grateful to witness such beauty. It's a breath of fresh air away from my computer.

"Wow..."

"Impressive, huh?"

River puts his bag on the ground. We don't really need artificial lights now. The moon is so high in the sky that it acts like a spotlight. I feel like I actually am, in the spotlight, and maybe that's as real as it is metaphorical, with what's happening to me at the moment.

"I didn't know you liked places like this," I murmur.

"When the lake is frozen, we sometimes train here with the team."

He pulls out a blanket for us to sit on, then looks contemplative.

"Are you interested in astronomy?"

What a strange question. I didn't know it mattered to him.

"I... uh... yes, a little. I mean, I didn't know you liked it."

"It's my favorite! I love it!"

Then it's more and more surprising. River is such an enigma to me. I usually love a mystery to solve, but now I'm wondering why he asked me to come here, why he's talking to me about this, why he's so close to me.

Why me? I'm nothing special and suddenly I feel like I've won some kind of lottery.

"Well, I... I didn't know you were into astronomy."

His air darkens a little. He pushes a stone with his foot.

"I'm a science buff, that's all."

I frown, then laugh.

"Right, yeah."

"I'm not kidding."

Oops. I may have struck a chord there.

"Ah er... I thought that..."

"That because I'm the captain of the hockey team, I don't have a brain?"

"No, no, that's not what..."

"It's all right, you don't need to say any more, Ava."

We remain silent for a few seconds, then I decide to defend myself.

"I'll point out that you said this was probably my first date. You had no idea."

"Was I wrong?"

He's got a point. I've always convinced myself that I wasn't interested in dating, and that sort of thing. The truth is, I've just never had the courage to take the plunge, and now, for the first time, I'm alone with a boy. The star of the campus, no less. It's quite something. I think it's the equivalent of taking your driving test in a Ferrari.

"I'm sorry, River. I didn't mean to hurt you."

"It's no big deal. I'm used to it. Don't worry."

I don't dare ask him the question and yet it burns my lips, but I'd like to know why. Why me rather than someone else? What does he like about me? Is he playing a game? It seems so impossible that a guy like him would be interested in me that... I start to doubt the reality of the moment we're living in. Still, he didn't bring me here to talk about team jerseys, that's for sure.

"Basically," he continues, "I wanted to go into science, you know."

"And... what stopped you?"

He bows his head slightly, then sighs.

"My dad. He always wanted to be a sportsman too, you see. Except he got injured when he was younger and now it's like he's pinned all his hopes on me to carry on the torch of his own dreams."

"Except that's not what you want?"

He shrugs casually.

"It's not horrible. I mean, I literally have everything I want. Everything. But... I confess that I'm more the type to ask myself existential questions, to read physics articles, to be interested in biology, and so on. Anyway... I'm not a sportsman at heart, so to speak."

I didn't expect that from him at all. I thought he was dumber than he is, and I blame myself for that.

"What's stopping you from studying it on the side?"

"It's not that simple. I don't want to like all this and find myself..."

"On the nerd side, right? I get it, yes. No need to say any more. I don't think it's necessary."

"I think it's cute."

"But you have a reputation to uphold?"

"That's just the way I am. Don't think it's a reputation. This is who I am now. I can't go back."

I see...

We're very different. We're really not from the same world, and yet tonight I feel we're getting closer.

"I get that. So... why did you want to come here with a geek like me?"

River shrugs, then smiles at me again.

"I don't know. I thought I'd give you a date to remember."

Now that's unforgettable...

"Well, uh... it's pretty successful."

"Do you know what happens at the end of a date?"

My heart beats a little faster because I have a vague idea of his answer.

"No..." I'm lying.

"Well, usually... people kiss."

My heart is about to burst from my chest. I'm on the verge of liquefying.

Without another word, River glues his lips to mine with perfect softness and harmony. I want to melt. I don't even realize what's happening, it's so unexpected and unhoped-for. I can't believe it's happening. I'm lost. Completely lost. What's going on here?

It's my very first kiss and... it's so perfect.

He doesn't try to force his way into my mouth. He takes his time, his hand gently caressing my cheek. His tongue slowly teases my lips, and I receive him full of apprehension, but also perfectly willing. Our mouths become one, and we're absorbed in a kiss that seems to last an eternity.

It's soft, warm, I'm transported and have a million butterflies in my stomach. They take off at full speed and don't stop, to the point where I feel like I'm nothing more than molten magma. Each of my extremities is like a dynamite barrel ready to explode, as if I were about to go off in a multitude of fireworks.

And then it all falls apart after the kiss. I can't help thinking of all the consequences that will follow.

Is it serious?

Does he like me?

And Bethany?!

I'm putting myself in a difficult situation.

7

"You haven't said a word all morning," Julia says to me while we're in the cafeteria.

I'm not hungry and I don't really want to talk.

"Ava?" asks Grace. "You didn't say how it went with the jerseys. How did it go?"

"And about your evening..." Julia insists.

Inevitably, she knows about the date I went on, and now that we've kissed, all I can think about is River. But should I tell them?

I stare at Julia, then at Grace, their attentive silence weighing on me. How can I explain this strange feeling I've had since that kiss? It's as if every thought, every heartbeat takes me back to River, to his smile, to the unexpected sweetness of his gesture. But I'm not ready to share that, not yet.

"The jerseys... We're making progress," I finally say, dodging the real question. "We've found a way to repair most of them by studying them one by one. That should do it. It... it went really well."

Julia stares at me, her piercing gaze weighing me down as if she's trying to read me. I know she's not fooled. She knows there's something more, something I'm not saying.

"It's good for the jerseys, Ava, but it's not really what I was asking you for..." she insists again.

I look down, playing with the edge of my tray. The truth is,

I don't know how to put into words what's happened between River and me. It's all new, all fragile. And if I say it out loud, it becomes real, and if it becomes real, then it can also fall apart. And also get me in trouble. Because damn it, if Bethany finds out... She already jumped down my throat when I was just talking to River, what's she going to do if she knows about our kiss?

"And... last night?" adds Grace, trying to bring me back to the conversation. "Did anything special happen?"

Julia raises an eyebrow with a satisfied smile, glad she doesn't have to pitch me again herself. She's looking forward to the answer, it seems.

I sigh because I can feel their expectation. They're not going to let it go, and part of me doesn't want to keep it to myself either. It's too big, too vibrant. Too unusual in my life as an invisible girl.

"Last night, River and I... we kissed," I say at last, my voice barely more than a whisper.

The silence that follows is palpable. I look up, fearing their reactions, but what I find in their eyes is not judgment, but curiosity, a hint of excitement even. They're absolutely thrilled, and I suddenly feel like I've become the coolest girl ever.

"Wow, really?"

Julia is the first to break the silence, a broad smile lighting up her face.

"Tell me about it!"

I bite my lip. Maybe sharing this with them won't be so terrifying. Maybe it'll even be a little liberating.

"It was... unexpected. He was there, and I was there, and then... it just happened. It was sweet, and a little awkward, but... perfect, in its own way. I feel... different."

"Where were you?"

"By the lake where the team trains when it's frozen."

"It must have been so romantic," insists Julia. "I didn't know River had a soft heart."

I don't think so, but I'm rather reassured that she thinks so.

"Well... yes, it was... it was really..."

Just as I'm telling the story, River and his buddies move into the cafeteria.

Julia and Grace exchange a glance, then, as if on cue, they turn to me, their eyes sparkling.

"It's so romantic, Ava," exclaims Grace, her voice full of enthusiasm. "Aren't you going to go see him?"

"Yes, but... I don't know what it means," I confess. "For River, maybe it was just a simple kiss, nothing more. I... I don't want to insist."

"Maybe, but maybe not," replies Julia, pragmatically. "The only way to find out is to see where it takes you. Don't get too carried away, but... don't close the door on what it might become either. What do you think? I feel like my little Ava is becoming a real woman!"

"Stop it!"

"He's the star of the campus! You're really not going to go see him?" Grace continues.

"Nooo... It would be so awkward if he just looks at me and asks what I want or why I am here..."

I risk a glance towards River's table, hoping my face doesn't betray the hurricane of emotions I'm feeling. Our eyes meet, and for a moment, the world around me fades away. His smile makes me melt. I quickly look away as I feel my cheeks flush.

"Look," murmurs Julia, a mischievous smile on her lips. "If it's not mutual, then I don't know what is."

Grace nods, clearly agreeing with Julia. I feel trapped by their encouragement, but in a strangely pleasant way.

"You didn't see anything," I protest weakly, even though my heart is pounding. "Nothing at all, okay?"

91

"Ava," Grace insists, "it's not every day you have a moment like this with someone like River. You should at least try, don't you think?"

"She's better at killing monsters online," agrees Julia. "Our Ava is a killer, but only in video games. In real life, she doesn't have an XP[3], does she?"

"That's it, yes," I confirm, pouting.

"But we agree you've just exchanged a peculiar look there, right?" continues Grace.

"No, we didn't look at each other in any particular way. It was more... you know... casual. Our eyes just met, that's all."

"No, I really think that..."

She is interrupted by River's unexpected arrival at our table. Julia and Grace exchange a knowing glance before making room for him. My heart races and I wonder if this is the moment to run away or face up to it.

"Hi," he says, looking at me with an intensity that makes me shiver. "I was hoping to see you."

Julia and Grace rise subtly, inventing an excuse to leave us alone. I suddenly feel exposed, but also curiously ready to face what's to come.

"Uh, hi," I retort, aware that my voice is trembling slightly. "I... I was just talking about..."

"About our moment at the lake?" He finishes my sentence, a mischievous smile lighting up his face. "I've been thinking about that a lot, too."

"No, I..."

"Finish your sentences, Ava. Stop letting others interrupt you. So, what did they say?"

I watch him, looking for signs of sincerity, wondering if he feels the same way I do. His presence is both intimidating and comforting.

---

3 XP are experience points in video games.

"They said it was very romantic and... I've thought about it too," I confess, encouraged by his attentive gaze.

I can feel Julia and Grace's curious glances from afar. But for the moment, none of that matters to me. I'm standing in front of River, and I have the feeling that all his friends are also looking at him with smiles on their faces.

Are they laughing at me?

"So, we're still on for the jerseys tonight?" says River, as if our mutual friends and curious onlookers no longer exist.

His question brings me back to the reality of our collaboration, but there's something in his voice that suggests it may not be just the jerseys he's interested in.

I nod, a little disconcerted by his close presence and obvious interest.

"Yes, of course. For the jerseys," I clarify, trying to keep my voice neutral despite the frantic beating of my heart.

My throat is so, so dry!

I swallow the large glass of water on my tray.

He inclines his head, his smile widening.

"Great. Great. And then... would you like to go out for a drink? Just you and me?"

His proposal is clear and direct, and I can feel his friends' eyes on us, some with amused smiles, others perhaps a little surprised.

Can they hear us from where they are? Is it a bet between them?

It's hard to tell.

I feel my cheeks flush even more, if that's possible.

"Uh, yes, why not," I manage to articulate, as my stomach loops.

River is being bold, and I wonder for a moment if I'm really ready for this. But then I remember his kiss, the unexpected softness of his lips against mine, and something inside me wants to explore where this might lead. The lake, the nature, the stars... all of it... it was so romantic.

"Cool. I'll meet you back here after the last class?"

I nod, suddenly unable to find any other words.

"Yes."

River stands up, ready to join his friends, but before he leaves, he leans forward slightly, his voice lowered so that only I can hear him.

"I really want to spend more time with you, Ava."

Then, without waiting for an answer, he walks away, leaving behind a scent of anticipation and excitement. I stand there transfixed, realizing that everyone has been watching us, including Julia and Grace, who return to the table with smiles that speak volumes. Instinctively, I glance around to make sure Bethany isn't around. If she were, she'd beat me up.

"So, is it official? Are you two dating now?" asks Julia, barely able to contain her enthusiasm.

I shake my head, trying to calm the whirlwind of my thoughts.

"I don't know," I murmur. "But I think I'm about to find out."

★ ★ ★

I'm not sure how to prepare for this jersey repair session with River. It's not like I've had any precise instructions about it.

For the moment, I'm still with Julia, in the bedroom. She sees me flailing around and I think she's really enjoying it - but I'm not!

"I don't know what to wear!" I grumble.

No matter how much I rummage through my closets, all I have are grandma's clothes. I feel like I'm 90!

"Why? I thought this was just a work session," she taunts

94

me.

"Gnagnagna, you know it's a bit more complicated than that, don't you?"

Julia bursts out laughing, clearly amused by my distress. She approaches and starts rummaging through my closet with me, uttering dramatic exclamations at every item of clothing she deems inappropriate for the occasion.

"Seriously, Ava, you have a way of turning a simple date into an existential crisis," she scoffs, pushing aside yet another dress I thought might not be so bad.

I sigh, dropping onto the bed, discouraged.

"I just... don't want to look like I've just come from a marathon library session, you know?"

"Oh, I can see perfectly well," she replies with a wink. "And for that, you need me. Prepare to be transformed, my dear. Tonight, River won't know what hit him."

She scurries off to her closet and returns a few minutes later with a selection of her own clothes. She places an outfit on my bed that seems to strike the perfect balance between casual and slightly seductive. A pair of skinny jeans to show off my legs, a slightly baggy but feminine top with discreet lace detailing, and a denim jacket to keep out the chill.

"Try this," she orders, a satisfied smile on her lips.

I change quickly, amazed at how well the outfit suits me and makes a welcome change from my eternal sweaters and shabby jeans. Julia then sits me down in front of the dressing table and tackles my hair with surprising dexterity.

"We'll just give you a few light waves," she decides, wielding the curling iron. "It'll give you a more... combed look, without overdoing it."

The result is amazing. The waves give sophisticated volume to my usually untamed hair, and I have to admit, I feel... pretty. Julia finishes it all off with a little mascara and a discreet gloss that highlight my eyes and lips without making me look like I've spent hours in the bathroom.

"Voilà," she congratulates herself, holding up a mirror. "The new Ava, ready to take on River and show him she's not just a geek. Come on, you're going to take out some cute boys tonight, and not just bad guys in front of a screen."

I can't help but smile, suddenly I feel so much more confident.

"Thank you, Julia. Seriously, I don't know what I'd do without you."

"You'd probably be hiding behind a sewing book right now," she jokes. "Go on, conquer that hockey player's heart. And remember, no matter what, you're amazing, just the way you are."

She's so nice. Even though I'm a little more confident, it's still River. And that's no small thing.

"But you're not coming to the sewing club?"

"Oh, no, everyone is waiting until you've finished deciding on the style and you've drawn the patterns to get started. Then it should go quickly."

I'm afraid it won't be ready in time... Coach Harrison said the game is coming up soon. I need to get organized.

"Oh, by the way! Here," she says, dipping her hand into her pocket.

I raise an eyebrow.

"What are you do...? No, Julia! Are you kidding me?!"

"Come on, it's only a condom!"

"But I won't need it!"

"Really? Who knows? You'd better go out covered, I don't want to find you knocked up!"

Upset, I grab the condom and slip it into my pocket.

Taking a deep breath - and cursing Julia a little - I leave the safety of our room and head for the sewing club, my heart pounding at the thought of meeting River again in a context so unfamiliar to both of us. The idea of working side by side on the jerseys, of sharing this space so familiar and yet so new with him, adds a layer of anticipation to my nervousness.

Arriving at the club, I find River already there, examining the damaged shirts with an air of seriousness I didn't know he had. His presence transforms the club's usually tranquil atmosphere into something more electric. Just the sight of him makes me liquefy.

"Hi, River," I say, trying to hide my apprehension under a layer of professionalism.

"Hey, Ava," he replies.

His eyes light up when he sees me.

I'm so fucking stressed.

"You look... incredible," River continues.

His simple but sincere compliment dispels some of my worries. I approach the tables where the jerseys are laid out, trying to concentrate on the task in hand.

"Then let's get started," I suggest. "We've got a lot of work to do if we want everything ready in time for your game."

River nods and we get to work. He watches me take the measurements, cut the backing fabrics, and adjust the patterns. To my surprise, he turns out to be an attentive and skilled student, following my instructions to the letter and quickly learning the basics of sewing.

"You're good at this," he says, a hint of admiration in his voice. "That's impressive."

I blush under his appreciative gaze, suddenly feeling more at ease in this shared exchange about my passion.

"Thank you, River. It's... it's sweet of you to pitch in so much."

"You know, I haven't forgotten that we have a date later on," he continues.

As we work, the conversation gets easier. Especially about what we've already shared. He tells me, of course, about my passion for video games and reminds me of his own, for science. He's truly amazing, and the more time passes, the more I enjoy being in his company.

The work session turns into a moment of unexpected complicity, strengthening the fragile bond that has begun to form between us. Despite the professional context of our meeting, there's an underlying tension, a shiver of excitement at the idea of what might come of this collaboration. At least on my side. But it's just that, sometimes, our hands brush against each other and there's a kind of spark. A kind of electricity in the air.

Why the hell does he think so much of me when I'm just a geek and he's the star of the campus? He even revealed some weaknesses to me. I don't think he tells everyone. It's so surprising.

"We did a great job! Thanks to you," he exclaims.

I can feel my heart racing against his intense gaze, and I wonder what else the evening has in store for us. Although the jersey repair was our excuse to get together, it's clear that we've woven something far more meaningful than thread through fabric. There's something else now, and I'm afraid to understand what.

After putting away the sewing equipment and taking a moment to admire our accomplished work, River turns to me with a smile that makes my heart beat a little faster.

"Ready for that drink?" he asks, a gleam of anticipation in his eyes.

I nod and my stomach knots at the thought of spending some one-on-one time with him in a more intimate setting.

We leave the sewing club and head for his room, located in one of the student residences on campus.

River's room is a surprising mix of order and his own passions. When he opens the door, I'm greeted by a spacious room, surprisingly tidy for a student. The walls are adorned with posters of hockey, famous scientists and a few video game illustrations, revealing a side of him I'm only beginning to understand. A desk laden with books and notes is neatly organized in one corner, next to a gaming PC that looks like it's been carefully customized.

We do have a few things in common, though, don't we?

"Welcome to my lair," he laughs, waving me in.

He walks over to a small fridge in another corner and pulls out two bottles of beer, handing me one of them. I take it, our fingers brushing briefly, and feel that spark of electricity between us again.

Come on, Ava, cheer up... think about what Julia gave you. But don't think about it too much. Rah... I am thinking about it! WAY TOO MUCH!

We sit on chairs opposite his desk, leaving the door ajar to let in the fresh air. River opens his beer with disconcerting ease and toasts lightly against mine.

"To an excellent working session, and to... what comes next," he exclaims, his gaze catching mine.

I toast with him, a little nervous, but excited by the turn of events. We start drinking, the conversation picking up where we left off at the sewing club. River shares stories about his hockey team, and how everyone treats Peter, the poor guy who always sits on the bench and brings the water glasses.

"Doesn't he have a role in the team?"

"No. He's pretty lame, but the coach keeps him around because he's an assistant, you know?"

"I think I'd be like him if I were in his place, I can't say I blame him," I laugh.

I admit I shouldn't make fun. People like Peter, or... like

me, are the ones who are usually targeted. But for once, I feel like I'm on the other side of the fence and have access to a whole new world of possibilities.

The beer helps lighten the mood, and soon we're laughing and sharing anecdotes like old friends. Yet beneath the laughter and smiles, there's a palpable tension, an attraction that neither of us seems ready to address directly.

We finally sit down on his bed, facing each other. I'm so nervous I feel like liquefying. He stares at me with such intensity that, if this continues, I might actually become liquid. He's too good to be true, but I'm a traumatized little creature. I feel like Bethany is there, lurking somewhere in the shadows, waiting to ambush me, to glare at me, or jump on me.

I try to banish this thought and as the evening progresses, I feel more and more at ease in his company, realizing that River is much more than the stereotypical seductive hockey player. He's complex, interesting and incredibly attentive. Granted, he's a playboy, but still... there's something else underneath his shell of charm.

When our eyes meet, there's a moment of silence, laden with unspoken words. River seems to hesitate, then leans slightly towards me, narrowing the space between us.

"Ava," he begins, his voice lower, more intimate. "I'm really glad you're here tonight."

Oh fuck, oh fuck, oh fuck...

My heart beats wildly, aware that this moment could define the beginning of something new and unexpected. I have Julia's words in mind.

"Me too, I had a great time this afternoon."

Once again, I hide behind my hair, but this time River doesn't let me. He gently untangles my hair.

"Why do you hide? I've noticed you do it a lot."

He... he noticed? Then he really does care about me, and

it's not an illusion. River likes me. Instinctively, I lean back slightly to step back, but suddenly I feel no resistance and fall backwards, out of bed. I hadn't calculated that the edge was so close. Damn student beds: they're so narrow!

"Ava! Are you OK?"

River rushes to my rescue and I suddenly understand why we don't put anything in the pockets of skinny jeans. Those pockets are SMALL. Small enough to let out a wild condom as you fall backwards.

"Yes, I..."

"Oh. I take it you had plans for tonight?"

I feel like dying. Right now. To disappear. I want to melt into the ground and never come out. To bury myself.

And I think River sees my discomfort. So, right away, he reassures me:

"Don't worry," he laughs. "It's nothing, really."

What possessed me to think that a guy like him could be interested in a girl like me? Of course, he thinks I'm ridiculous. He'll kick me out.

But instead, River grabs my hand and helps me up, before pulling me against him.

Our mouths are almost glued together and my whole body is just waiting for yesterday to happen again. My whole being is crying out for it. It can't wait any longer. Impatience is eating away at me.

"Is that what you want?" he murmurs.

My heart is racing. My brain doesn't know what to say. It's as if it no longer has any control over my mouth, which, without me having to think about it, answers: "yes".

The smile on River's face is as adorable as it is sexy. And from that moment on, I understand that he's the one who's going to take charge. I've got to be up to it, I don't want to look like an apprentice - yet that's what I am. He's got to be pretty experienced, and all I know about sex is from the Internet. Then again, I'm not sure that's a realistic view of things. So, OK, I've talked to Julia a bit about it, but that doesn't mean I'm an expert - because she isn't either. She's had a first time and that's it. We're not great seductresses.

"Make yourself comfortable," River says.

Come on, relax, Ava, because damn it, you're going to do it!

I can't believe I'm actually going to sleep with River Ashton. This can't be happening! I must be in a dream I'm going to wake up from soon.

The next thing I know, River is standing over me. We're still dressed, and my heart is racing as I feel his mouth against mine. His kisses are so soft they make velvet look like plaster. I'm back in his room, in his bed, and his body is now stretching over mine.

His gaze pierces me like a long sewing needle and I shudder, he is so handsome. He wants me as much as I want him. I can see it in his eyes.

He slowly strips me, while I undress him. My whole body trembles. I'm at the height of my arousal and before long, we're under the comforter for foreplay, during which I ask myself a lot of questions.

He's so perfect. His body is so well sculpted. Is mine exciting enough? Am I good enough for him? Will this lead to a lasting relationship? What does it mean to him?

But when he lays his hands on me. When he grazes my intimacy with all the gentleness, he's capable of, I can't hold back my moans. He's driving me crazy, so I try to put on a brave face and make the best of it, too. This is the first time I've touched a man's sex, but from his grunts, I'd say I'm not doing too badly.

I feel more confident, and I let myself enjoy this interlude in my life.

"Have you done this before?" he asks breathlessly. Without giving me time to respond, he continues: "Because you do it so well."

Once the temperature has risen solidly, we get down to business. River grabs the condom I've left on the floor, then tears it off, with a smile.

"It will come in handy, after all."

That's all I was hoping for, and without even bothering to answer, I pull him against me again. I want to feel him. Inside me. I want us to be as close as possible, to each other. I'm not the kind of person who gives up so easily, but with him, I could forget the whole world, because he provokes feelings in me that I never thought I'd feel. I've always thought that relationships like this weren't for me. That I'd end up getting married on World of Warcraft[4] and that would be fine. That I'd never experience desire, passion, torrid moments like this, and River shows me that I was wrong.

"I'm not hurting you?" he asks gently.

I shake my head negatively as he slowly sinks into me. I can't avoid a grimace, and he stops, giving me time to get used to him.

"You... you can go on..." I say to give him the signal that everything's OK.

At first, the pain seems severe, and I don't think I can take it. But his gentle insistence gets the better of my body, and I end up finding pleasure in it. He slides in and out of me, slowly consuming me. My moans get louder and louder, but our lovemaking remains calm. River isn't a brute - which is just as well. Every one of his muscles ripples insolently above me, transporting me.

I'm on the verge of exploding. Because of his mouth, because of his hands, because of what he's doing to me below. All

---

4 Video game set in a medieval fantasy world.

of this creates a cocktail that sends a jolt of pleasure through my lower abdomen and up to the back of my neck. I don't think I've ever felt anything like it, because for the first time, I'm cumming. For real. With a man.

Out of breath, I shift to the side once we've finished, and River gives me a tender look. I don't feel like talking, I just want to snuggle up to him. I think we have a lot more in common than I imagined, and that pleases me a lot. I was wrong about him.

He's an athlete, yes. But from now on, he's mine.

I'm still overwhelmed when I wake up this morning. Even if, once again, it's Julia who pulls me out of my dreams.

"Mmmh... what's going on?"

"Well, we've got to get ready for class!"

"Ah, yes..."

I'm struggling to wake up, but luckily, she's already made coffee for me.

"So... looks like you got in late last night."

At the mere mention of these words, I blush.

"Yes, uh... it was... well, you know how it is, right?"

"Spending part of the night with River Ashton? No, I haven't the faintest idea," she laughs.

"Shush! Not so loud!"

"Who can hear us?"

I still have this unpleasant feeling that the walls have ears, and now I'm wary of Bethany. I've had such a magical time that I feel like I'm in a bubble and I feel like it could burst at any moment. What if that cheerleader moth somehow got wind of it? That would be horrible. She'd throw me into the snake pit - by which I mean her group of friends - so they could make fun of me. I don't know if I can really have a lasting relationship with River. But I owe it to myself to try! In the name of all the lost girls in the world, I've got to give it a try! Not all of us are lucky enough to date the handsome campus

105

star and captain of the hockey team. I barely realize what happened yesterday and I'm trying to brush it off with Julia.

"And then nothing happened, you see, so..."

"Liar!"

"What?! But why are you..."

"Because I went through your pants! And I couldn't find the condom. So, unless you made water bombs with it, I think you've got something to tell me, don't you?"

Trapped. She's way too smart for me!

Since that's the way it is, I decide to let loose and recount everything in great detail. As I speak - during our morning preparation - Julia makes little mouth circles. I can see she's having trouble believing her ears, and yet I'm only telling the truth.

"What about size?"

"Size?"

"Yeah, you know, some..."

"Hey! Stop it, that's private!"

She bursts out laughing, then resumes:

"OK, OK, I see: now that he's your boyfriend, you want to protect his privacy? It's a credit to you."

The mere mention of 'boyfriend' makes my cheeks turn pink.

Once we're ready, we leave the room for class, and this time I'm more relaxed and confident than ever. I can't wait to see River again. I've never had a boyfriend before. It's all new to me.

We're strolling through the corridors, heading for class, when I spot him. My heart leaps in my chest.

Seeing him, all the moments we shared last night flash through my mind, every smile, every touch, intensifying the excitement of seeing him again. I approach, a shy but hopeful smile stretching my lips. River is surrounded by some of his teammates, deep in animated conversation, but he turns to me as soon as he sees me.

"Hello, Ava," he says with a friendly smile (the kind you reserve for a good acquaintance, nothing more). "How are you this morning?"

His voice is warm, but there's a distance, an invisible barrier that I didn't expect to feel. I blink, a little bewildered, trying to hold on to the idea that maybe, after all, I've been fooling myself.

"Uh, hi, River. I'm fine, how are you?"

My voice trembles slightly, betraying my inner turmoil.

"Great, great. Last night was fun," he says, before quickly turning to his friends to continue their previous discussion.

The exchange is brief, polite, but there's no hint of what happened between us, no sign that our night together has changed anything for him. My heart tightens. I had imagined... hoped even that this morning would mark the beginning of something special between us, but it seems that for River, I'm just a good friend, a project partner, nothing more. At best, a one-night stand or a trophy.

I stand there for a moment, transfixed, as River and his friends walk away, resuming their conversation as if nothing had happened. The reality of the situation gradually dawns on me: last night, as intimate and meaningful as it was for me, was just another pleasant moment for River.

"Are you all right, Ava?" asks Julia as she joins me. "Everything went well with River."

I'm almost speechless. I can't get a word out, but I finally do after a few moments of silence.

"Yes. I'm fine. Excuse me, I have to go to the bathroom..."

I rush to the nearest toilet, my throat tight, my eyes burning with tears that I refuse to let flow in front of the others. Once I've locked the door behind me, I lean against the cold wall, and finally let my emotions overwhelm me. The tears flow freely, marking warm furrows on my cheeks, as I desperately try to catch my breath between sobs.

I can't believe it, I'm an idiot! How stupid can I be, it's not possible to be that stupid... I should have known better; I should have seen it coming. He fucks girls all the time. It doesn't mean anything to him, but I was starting to get attached. I was... I don't know... I felt good with him.

I don't know how long I stand there, curled up inside myself, silently mourning the loss of an illusion. It's the pain of having opened my heart, of having believed in something more, only to realize that I wasn't on the same wavelength as River.

The bathroom door opens slowly, and I hear Julia's voice, full of concern.

"Ava? Are you here?"

I sniffle, trying to hide the traces of my tears with the back of my hand.

"Yes," I murmur, my voice hoarse with tears.

Julia approaches and sits down next to me on the cold floor. She doesn't say anything for a while, just gives me a hug. Her presence is a soothing balm, and little by little, my sobs subside.

"What's going on, Ava? Why are you crying?"

I feel torn at the thought of sharing my pain, but at the same time, I know I can't hide anything from him.

"It's River," I begin, my voice trembling. "I thought that... that what happened last night meant something to him. But this morning, he was just... friendly. Like nothing special had happened."

Julia remains silent for a moment, then sighs.

"Ava, I'm so sorry. Guys like River, they... they don't always think about the consequences of their actions. Especially when it comes to feelings."

I nod and my tears begin to flow again.

"I feel so stupid. I thought we had... something special."

"You're not stupid, Ava. You're human. You're allowed to feel things, to get attached. But sometimes, others aren't in the same place as us, and that hurts. What you feel is valid, never forget that. River... is River."

Julia's words are a small comfort in the whirlwind of pain and confusion that surrounds me. She stays with me, holding my hand, until I feel strong enough to wipe away my tears and consider leaving the bathroom.

"Thank you, Julia. I don't know what I'd do without you," I say, my voice still fragile.

"You'll never have to find out," she replies with a sad smile. "Shall we go to class? We'll get killed if we don't."

We leave the bathroom. As I enter the classroom, I feel the curious glances of some of my classmates, but I concentrate on my notes, trying to lose myself in the teacher's explanations. However, the words seem to float away from me, and I struggle to keep my mind focused on the lesson rather than the pain in my heart. I shouldn't let it get to me like this. After all, we didn't promise each other anything.

The day stretches on, long and painful. Every time I pass River in the corridors or in class, a weight forms in my stomach, and I look away, unable to cope with his apparent indifference. Julia remains by my side, a comforting presence, even if she can't completely ease my grief. Only video games can, I think.

At lunchtime, as I'm secluded in a corner of the cafeteria with a barely eaten sandwich, Grace approaches me shyly. She seems rather enthusiastic.

"Hey, Ava," she begins softly. "I just wanted to let you know that we're going to start working on the jerseys this afternoon. Coach Harrison says the game is coming up fast, and he'd like to get everything ready very quickly."

I look up at her, realizing that, despite my personal grief, I can't abandon the sewing club and the commitments I've made. The other members are counting on me, and these shirts represent much more than a simple project: they're the culmination of our teamwork, our collective efforts.

"Thank you, Grace, I... I'll be there, of course."

Grace smiles gently at me, placing a comforting hand on my shoulder.

"Cool! Besides, you've got a lot to tell us, haven't you?"

Not so much, actually.

"Yeah, ahah..."

★ ★ ★

Soon after class, I still have a bitter taste in my mouth: disappointment. I head off to the sewing club, as we still have some shirts to repair. Despite my experience with River, I still have to face up to the responsibilities I've taken on in front of the coach.

The atmosphere in the workshop is focused and creative. Piles of jerseys are waiting to be sewn, and club members are already bustling around the worktables. I try to focus solely on the task in hand, putting aside my personal emotions to concentrate on the repair patterns I've prepared.

I unfold the sketches and detailed instructions on a large table, checking every detail to make sure nothing has been forgotten. It's an important project for the club and for me, a chance to prove that I can manage my professional responsibilities, even when the personal becomes complicated. And then, if the coach keeps his word, we'll be able to get financing...

This is the moment River chooses to enter the room in his

turn. Julia glares at him, but I try to remain perfectly neutral and focus on what I have to do.

"Here are the patterns for the repairs," I announce to the group. "I've tried to find the best solution for each damage without compromising the integrity of the original design."

The club members gather to examine the plans, expressing their approval and enthusiasm for the project in turn. Mark, who always has a critical eye for detail, scans the patterns carefully before looking up at me.

"It's good work, Ava, but we seem to be short of certain materials to apply your repairs. We're going to need more reinforced thread and some of those specific patches you mentioned here," he points out, pointing to my notes.

My heart misses a beat. In the whirlwind of emotions of the last few days, I neglected to check our inventory and make sure we had everything we needed. I bite my lip, frustrated by my lack of foresight.

"You're right, Mark. Sorry, I should have checked that first. I'll take care of finding what we need," I say, determined to rectify my mistake.

"We'll have to go and buy all this stuff," mumbles Julia.

"I'll go. I'm the one who forgot, so..."

"Where is it?" asks River.

Everyone turns to him and tries not to look nervous.

"Well, uh... not exactly next door," I retort.

I try to remain dignified, but deep down I'm angry.

"Great. How do we do it?" asks Grace.

"I'll ask the coach. I'm sure he'll have a plan," says River.

Suddenly, I'm a little afraid of how things might turn out.

River and I make our way to Coach Harrison's office, a tense silence between us. Despite the uncomfortable situation, part of me is grateful for his initiative. Arriving in front of the office, River knocks and we enter at Harrison's invitation.

"Coach, we've got a problem with the jerseys. We're short of material for the repairs, and it looks like we'll have to go and buy them," explains River in a tone that betrays his irritation at the idea of this unexpected chore.

Coach Harrison looks at each of us in turn, his eyes finally settling on River.

"All right. It's your duty as captain to make sure the team has everything it needs. You're going to take Ava so she can buy what's missing. It's important for the team. Do you understand me?"

River bellows, clearly unhappy with this turn of events.

"Coach, are you serious? I'm..."

"No 'buts', River. It's a question of responsibility. You're the captain, that's part of your role," cuts in the coach in a tone that leaves no room for negotiation. "Besides, we both know why this little mishap happened, don't we? Hmm?"

River glances in my direction, his eyes expressing a mixture of resignation and frustration.

"All right, then. Let's go," he finally says. "Damn..."

I still don't say a word. I'm so upset by River's behavior that I hardly dare say a word.

We leave the coach's office and head for River's car.

"How are you?" he asks as we settle into the car. "You seem a little distant."

I'm the one who's distant?!

I hope he's kidding.

"Are you kidding?"

"What?"

"River! What happened yesterday!"

He turns to me in surprise. Is he deliberately not understanding what I want to say?

"We slept together," I announce.

"Yeah. I know I was there. And?" he asks.

"Doesn't that mean anything to you?"

He shrugs, and once again, I feel like my heart is cracking into a thousand pieces.

"What do you want me to say, Ava?"

His hands are firmly gripped around the steering wheel.

"I... I don't know that... that matters to you?"

He doesn't answer, and suddenly I understand: he doesn't care at all. For him, it was just a game. He wanted to see if he could bang the uptight geek, and now that he's succeeded, he's moving on.

"Is it true that you were banging a girl in the showers? And that's why the t-shirts were vandalized?"

River sighs heavily.

"Yeah. I seriously screwed up; I know."

"You don't care, do you?"

"What the hell are you talking about?"

I prefer not to say anything. I just lean against the window, waiting. The store is nowhere near, and the coach has given us some money. An advance on what he'll give us, after the repairs.

"I don't like these dark clouds very much..." says River.

I glance up at the sky, and it's true that the weather is beginning to look bad.

As we approach the store, large black clouds have gathered above us, and suddenly a downpour of rain falls on the vehicle. River increases the speed of the windshield wipers.

"Listen, Ava," River begins, his voice almost covered by the sound of rain hitting the windshield. "I didn't want to... well, I didn't want to make you feel like it didn't mean anything."

I turn my head towards him, surprised by his admission. The rain creates a veil that seems to isolate our world from the rest, forcing us to face the situation here and now.

"So, what was it?" I ask, my voice trembling.

"I don't know. I'm confused. I don't want to hurt you, but I'm not sure what I want either. It's complicated, that's all."

He's just trying to keep up appearances for his jock friends.

His answer doesn't bring the comfort I'd hoped for, but it does open a door to the complexity of his feelings, something I hadn't considered before. The reality of our situation, complicated and tangled, dawns on me.

We arrive at the store in a rainstorm, running across the parking lot to shelter from the rain. The inside of the store is warm and dry, in stark contrast to the storm outside. We set about the task of finding all the necessary equipment, the rain outside serving as a backdrop to our shared mission.

Finally, with all the materials in hand, we wait at the checkout, and I pay with the dollars the coach left us.

Still no word. Almost no word. I have a feeling we're still on the outs. At least a little.

We get back into the car, still running.

"Look at that," says River, looking out the driver's window at the sky. "It's too stormy to drive right now. We could have an accident. It's dangerous. It's going to fall like hell, and you don't want to be here when it does."

I glance outside and, indeed, the storm seems to be intensifying, with lightning streaking across the sky with increasing frequency. The thunder rumbles loudly. And as if that wasn't enough, night begins to fall, shrouding the parking lot in an ominous darkness.

"Maybe we should wait it out," suggests River. "We can stay here for a while. It should calm down soon."

I nod. River starts the car and finds a place to park a little out of the way, where we can watch the storm in safety. He cuts the engine, and suddenly the only sound is that of rain drumming against the roof of the car. We're in a motel parking lot.

The atmosphere in the car is strangely peaceful, despite the storm outside. The tension between us seems to have dissipated, replaced by a kind of tacit truce. River plays absent-mindedly with the car key, his eyes fixed on the fogged-up windshield.

"You know, I've never really liked thunderstorms," he says suddenly. "But there's something... I don't know, exhilarating about watching them, especially when you're safe inside."

I look at him, astonished by this unexpected confession.

"I like thunderstorms," I retort. "They remind me that there are things much bigger than our little problems."

River turns his head towards me, a half-smile on his lips.

"That's one way of looking at it."

We stand there, watching the storm together, talking intermittently about everything and nothing. It's a strangely intimate moment, shared in the cocoon of the car, far from the complications of our relationship. For once, it seems we can just be two people, without expectations or disappointments.

That said, it's not letting up. Not at all, in fact. It's as if, instead of calming down, the storm is only intensifying. We'll never get out of it.

To chase away boredom - or fear? - River turns on the radio, where the news is playing. They're talking about the coming storm, and it's not looking good.

The newscaster's voice on the radio is deep and urgent. It cuts through the noise of the rain, which is pounding even harder against the car.

"We inform you that a severe storm is underway and is expected to intensify in the coming hours. We advise everyone to take shelter as soon as possible. There is a risk of flooding and power cuts. Please exercise caution and avoid unnecessary travel."

River and I exchange a worried glance. The relaxed atmosphere of a moment ago has given way to palpable tension. The storm is no longer a fascinating spectacle, but a real threat to our safety.

And shit, it had to happen now. And with Julia texting me...

★ **Julia:** *Where are you?!*
★ **Ava:** *Stuck in the car because of the storm. I don't know what we're going to do!*

"We can't go back," River murmurs, his gaze fixed on the outside where visibility has been considerably reduced.

He's right. The idea of trying to get back to campus in this storm is unthinkable. The risk of accident is far too high.

"There's always the motel," he suggests after a moment's silence. "We could take shelter there until things calm down. Sounds good?"

Again, I nod. While the idea of spending even more time, alone, with River in a motel adds a layer of complexity to our already complicated situation, safety is our priority.

"Ready to run to the motel?"

Strangely, he looks almost amused.

"Not at all."

"And yet, we're going to have to get going."

He takes off his jacket. What the hell is he doing?!

"Here," he says, handing it to me. "Put it over your head."

"But what about you...?"

"Go!"

At his signal and without waiting for my reply, River dashes off. I follow without flinching - cursing the damn rain all the same. We run at full speed across the parking lot, then rush inside the motel, soaking wet despite the short distance between the car and the entrance. The reception is warm, a haven of peace compared to the chaos outside. River takes care of booking a room while I stand there, shivering, my clothes sticking to my skin. It's a good thing he gave me his jacket. Otherwise, my hair would have been soaked. That would have been really unpleasant.

With the key in hand, we make our way upstairs to our temporary room in uncomfortable silence. The reality of our situation, stuck together in a motel because of a storm, suddenly seems very real.

The room is basic but comfortable, with a large double bed. I swallow hard but try to keep calm. River is the first to break the silence.

"I'll get some dry towels and food. Is there anything you need?"

I shake my head, my mind still occupied by recent events and the interrupted conversation in the car.

"No, I'm fine, thanks."

As River leaves, I sit on the bed and my thoughts swirl. This night, unexpected and forced by the storm, could be a chance to clear things up between us. Or it might not. Only time will tell.

For the moment, I'm concentrating on the soothing sound of the rain against the window.

★ **Julia:** *Are you safe?*

Julia again.

★ **Ava:** *Yes. We've found a shelter. We won't be back tonight.*
★ **Julia:** *Where?*

If I tell her, she's going to tease me until the end of time, but I don't really have a choice.

⋆ **Ava:** *A motel*
⋆ **Julia:** *Ohhhhhh! What great news! You two get to spend some time together! Isn't that nice?*

I furiously want to tell her to shut up, but I don't dare. God, I wish I had my computer!

⋆ **Ava:** *Nothing's going to happen!*
⋆ **Julia:** *Unless you decide otherwise. And use the condom I slipped into your wallet.*

She did what?!

⋆ **Ava:** *Are you kidding me?!*

Out of curiosity, I decide to check and almost turn a blind eye when I realize she's slipped a condom into my things.

As soon as I hear River return, I close my wallet and hurriedly tuck it into my pocket.

"Well, they only had snacks, so the meal will be a bit... calorific," he laughs as he places packets of chips and candy on the bed.

And then, a great silence follows. I wonder what River has in mind, but for now, he settles in by turning on the TV - which doesn't work.

"I don't think we're in a five-star hotel," he comments with a sigh.

"That's for sure."

"Is everything okay?"

Tell him? Not to tell him?

"Not really."

He raises an eyebrow, looking surprised.

"What do you mean?" he asks.

"I don't know where... where we are, really."

River turns off the television - which crackles - a sign that he's giving me his full attention, which only makes me more nervous. I feel vulnerable, naked, but I know that if I don't speak up now, I may never get the chance.

"After what happened between us, I just feel... lost. You act like nothing happened, like we were just friends. But for me, it was more than that," I begin, my voice trembling.

River runs a hand through his hair, clearly uncomfortable with the direction of our conversation.

"Ava, I... I'm sorry. I screwed up. I thought it was just a... a one-time thing. I didn't mean to get your hopes up," he admits.

His admission hurts me, but at the same time, I appreciate his honesty. However, it's not enough to ease the pain of feeling insignificant in his eyes.

It's now or never. I've got to tell him. And not stay on a possible regret of not having spoken...

"But I like you, River. More than I ever imagined. And I hate feeling like this, like I'm just another girl on your list. It makes me feel... used."

River seems shocked by my words, and for the first time I see a glimmer of regret in his eyes.

"I didn't want you to feel used. I didn't mean to. And I hate knowing I made you feel that way," he murmurs.

He moves closer, hesitating for a moment before taking my hand. His touch is both comforting and heartbreaking, as it reminds me of what I thought was possible between us. I'm not sure I want to... to go any further. But on the other hand, it's so tempting.

"I... I like you, Ava. It's a feeling I haven't completely understood myself. I know it's unfair to you, this uncertainty, but I... I don't want to lose you, either."

These words surprise me. They don't solve everything, but they open a door I thought was closed forever. Maybe River is as confused as I am, maybe there's a chance for us to navigate this complexity together. It's all so strange.

"I don't know where this is going, River. But I need to know that this... that we matter to you. That I'm not just a one-night stand," I retort.

River squeezes my hand, nodding slowly.

"It matters. You matter to me, Ava. And I'm willing to do whatever it takes to prove that to you. Give me a chance to fix this."

In the motel, far from everyone and everything, under the distant sound of the rain that has resumed, we meet at a crossroads. River's words bring a semblance of hope, a glimmer in the darkness of my doubts and fears.

"How?" I ask.

Instead of answering me, and because a gesture is worth a thousand words, River places a kiss on my lips with a tenderness I didn't know he had. I want to jump all over him. To describe all the passion I feel for him, but I can't. I can't move, I'm paralyzed by the gentleness of his movements. I let myself be carried away. Caught up in the game.

But this time, I want to be in control, and I come to my senses, realizing what's happening.

Will Julia's condom save my life once again?!

I don't know. But I feel that the situation could get out of hand at any moment.

"I like you so much," admits River, taking off my top.

And without giving me the slightest respite, he continues to devour my lips, as if his life depends on it. I love this sensual bestiality. I never thought it would happen to me. Not like this. The two of us, stuck in this motel with a crackling TV and nothing but passion to occupy us. But there's a kind of sincerity I'm unable to overlook, in River. He's sweet. He's passionate. He wants it. I sense that it's not just about sex. It goes way beyond that.

I let him strip me with all the gentleness he's capable of, and since I don't want to be passive, I do the same with him. It's out of the question for him to be in full control of the situation this time - even if, I must admit, it's not unpleasant.

We spread out on the bed without separating from each other for a moment. It's both fusional and harmonious. The sensation of his body against mine is a delight I could quickly become addicted to.

He kisses my neck passionately, then slides his hand closer and closer to my intimacy. Immediately, a wave of pleasure washes over me.

"I have a feeling we're going to go too far and wish we had the protection we need to do it," he murmurs.

I've got just the thing.

"Wait a minute. I've got something."

"Did you plan this?" he smiles.

"Are you accusing me of organizing a rain dance so that we'd be trapped in a storm? I wish I had that power, but I don't."

River laughs, then, without further words, lets his body speak instead of his mouth - which is otherwise more exciting. I love it when he's like that, on top of me. There's nothing hotter, and already I feel I'm losing control. I'm invaded by an immense heat. He makes me feel good. Between his muscular arms, I feel as if the world around me no longer exists and there's only us. Just him and me, letting out all the bestiality we hide from the rest of the world.

I'm ecstatic and hope we don't have any neighbors. Otherwise, they might complain. I'm almost a little ashamed, but boy, does it feel good to make love to him. I had no idea I liked him so much, but more importantly, I had no idea that he was so into me. All my geeky dreams came true in one fell swoop. For once, this is my romance. My story.

Once we've finished, I snuggle into his arms, while he strokes my hair.

"So... was it more than just sex for you?" I ask.

"Of course. What do you think?"

With his playboy reputation... he can't blame me for asking.

"I don't know, River... you... well... you have quite a reputation, so..."

"What's it to you? Do you think I could hurt you?"

"No. Well, I hope not."

He sighs heavily. I know what's on his mind. Of course he doesn't want to hurt me, but on the other hand, there are the others. The look in their eyes. His attitude this morning spoke for itself.

"Do you want... you and me to be together?" he asks.

I look up at him, surprised by his question.

"What... what?"

"For real, I mean."

"Are you serious?"

"Ava, I find you so interesting. And yet, you're always hiding."

"Is that supposed to be a compliment?"

"Of course it is. The most beautiful diamonds tend to hide in plain sight. Your body is magnificent, but your mind is an exceptional jewel."

Now I'm melting. He's literally asking me to be his girlfriend.

"I... I..."

"You're worried, aren't you?"

"A little. I'm afraid of the others. I'm afraid of being told all the time that you and I don't belong in the same world."

"We don't care about the others, okay? They're not the

ones who matter."

"Okay, hidden nerd, I'll make a note," I retort.

"It's not that... it's just that... Yeah, I have a bit of trouble with what other people think, the way they look at me," he admits.

I frown.

"For someone as exposed as you, it's amazing."

"You talk too much. Shouldn't I shut you up?" he laughs.

"Does it bother you that I'm talking, or that I'm right?"

"If you continue, I'll kiss you."

"So, I'm going to continue on purpose."

River doesn't hesitate. He approaches me gently, his gaze locked in mine, and places a kiss on my lips. It's a gentle, exploratory kiss at first, which quickly becomes more passionate, more assertive. There's a silent promise in this gesture, an acceptance of everything we are, with our fears, our hopes and our differences. Him, the great athlete, and me, the shy geek. It's not going to work out. True enough. Still, I really want to give it a try. I don't know what it all means between us, but I feel it could go further. Maybe we both have a future, even if it's uncertain.

The warmth of his kiss dispels my last reservations. In this moment, nothing else exists but the two of us. Doubts about our different worlds, fears of judgment, all evaporate in the face of the certainty of what I feel for him.

I like him. Far too much. It's almost scary.

When we finally part, breathless, I look at him with a shy smile.

"You're really cute. You know that, Carrot?"

We spend the rest of the evening talking, laughing and planning our immediate future. There's still a lot to discover about each other, obstacles to overcome, but for the first time in a long time, I feel optimistic about the future. Because I'm with him. Because he's shown me that all this means more than... sex.

The night at the motel, away from the storm and outside scrutiny, becomes a refuge, a haven where we can simply be ourselves. And it feels so good!

"You know, our next game, the one for which the jerseys have to be ready..." River says after a moment's silence, breaking the comfortable tranquility that had settled between us. It's a big game, and... I hope you'll come and see me play."

I'm a little surprised by his invitation, not because of its content, but because of the importance it seems to have for him. It's as if he's asking me to be part of his world, not just as a friend or confidante, but as someone important to him. It's an offer I can't refuse. It seems to mean a lot to him.

"Of course I'll be there, River. I wouldn't miss it for the world."

A smile lights up his face, dispelling any remaining shadows of doubt.

"It means a lot to me, Carrot. It really does. Thank you, Carrot! You'll see, we'll do great. The team and I have been preparing all season. All we need is your hard work, and we'll be perfect!"

The rest of the evening passes in a bubble of shared happiness. We talk about everything and nothing, share laughs and comfortable silences, but eventually the day's fatigue catches up with us, and we settle down to sleep, the soothing sound of the rain falling outside serving as my lullaby.

Lying in his arms, I feel incredibly good, pampered, and safe. The storm outside seems far away, mere background noise compared to the warmth and tranquility I find here, with him. My anxieties and fears seem to have subsided, at least for the moment, replaced by a feeling of peace.

"Good night, Carrot," River murmurs.

Am I dreaming or... is his voice really tinged with affection?
"Good night, secret nerd," I retort with a smile in my voice.

I fall asleep quickly, lulled by the steady rhythm of his breathing and the deep feeling of being exactly where I'm supposed to be. For the first time in a long time, I feel complete, a new and deliciously frightening feeling.

9

Morning light filters through the curtains as I gently feel River shake me awake. My eyes open to his smiling face. He holds two steaming cups of coffee in one hand and a small paper bag in the other. He's managed to find a place open early in the morning to bring us breakfast.

"Hello, Carrot. I found a café open not far from here. I hope you like black coffee," he says, handing me one of the cups.

I sit up, still a little sleepy, and accept the coffee gratefully. And I can't help but smile at his thoughtful gesture.

"Thank you, River. It's perfect," I whisper, savoring the first sip.

He sits down next to me on the bed, opening the bag to reveal some delicious-looking pastries. I'm not used to having instant energy when I wake up. I'm usually exhausted from an evening of knitting or gaming the night before. So, inevitably, I wake up with bags under my eyes, but this time... I slept pretty well.

"I thought we could have a nice breakfast before going home," he adds, handing me a pastry.

We eat in silence for a few moments, the comfort of the previous night still enveloping the room. It's strange how simple gestures can transform an ordinary moment into something special.

"The rain has stopped. We should have no trouble getting back to campus now," he announces once we've finished eating.

I nod, a little sad that our out-of-time parenthesis has to come to an end, but also eager to get back to our new reality, the one where River and I are officially together.

"I can't wait to see you play at the game," I confess, reminding him that I'll be there to support him, no matter what others might think or say.

"It means a lot to me, Carrot. It really does. Knowing you'll be there... makes me want to win even more."

We finish breakfast and prepare to leave the motel. On the way out, I feel invigorated, ready to take on the world with River by my side. The promise of the future, despite its uncertainties, suddenly seems full of possibilities. And as we make our way to the car, hand in hand, I can't help but feel good, loved, and safe, with the soothing sound of the rain having stopped and the sun beginning to break through the clouds.

I look at my phone and see that Julia has HARASSED me with messages.

I decide to reply to her while River starts the car and heads for campus. My fingers fly across the screen, eager to share with her the events of the last few hours. Because it's been crazy!

★ **Ava:** *Julia, you can't imagine what's been going on! River and me. I think we really like each other... I'll tell you all about it when I see you!*

I write, and the smile can't leave my lips. Julia's response is swift, a flood of enthusiastic and curious messages flooding my phone, she's clearly eager to hear every little detail.

★ **Julia:** *Are you kidding me?!*
★ **Julia:** *Girl, answer me!*
★ **Julia:** *Hello, Ava, has the condom been used?*
★ **Julia:** *I repeat: has Captain Condom done his job?*

Damn, I'm going to have to be honest, but on the other hand, she's fun, so, I answer:

★ **Ava:** *Yes!*
★ **Julia:** *I knew it!*

I can't hold back a chuckle.
"What's so funny?" asks River with a smile.
"Julia."
"Ah, yes, your friend... I hope you're not telling her everything in detail, are you?"
I press my phone against my chest with a mischievous look on my face.
"Mmh... not in detail, but a little."
He bursts out laughing. With him, I feel I can be myself, and that's priceless.
The drive to campus is a bubble of contentment. River and I exchange knowing glances and smiles, while soft music from the radio fills the short silences. The tension and uncertainty that had accompanied us to the motel seem to dissolve, replaced by a sense of closeness and burgeoning trust. I'm over the moon!
As we arrive, the campus is bathed in golden morning light, students already hurrying to their first classes of the day. River parks, and before getting out of the car, he turns to me, taking my hand in his.
"Thanks for being there, Carrot. It's been great."
I feel my heart skip a beat.

129

"See you at the game. I'll be there to support you!"

"I'm pretty sure we'll see each other before, though."

"I guess you're right. Anyway, we've got some work to finish on the jerseys..."

My legs are shaky. I quickly make my way to my next class. I can't believe I'm flirting with a boy. Me! By the time I arrive, I've already spotted Julia waiting for me with a look of anticipation painted on her face. As soon as our eyes meet, she pounces on me.

"Ava! Tell me all about it! I want to know everything!" she exclaims, unable to contain her excitement.

And off I go, unpacking every detail for her, from beginning to end, from the moment River and I were caught in the storm to our farewell this morning. She listens so intently that for a moment I think she almost takes out the popcorn.

This is a new chapter for me, and I can't wait to see where it takes us. I think we can really build something. I think he likes me.

"It's so amazing and... so cute," she adds. "Ahhh, I'm almost jealous! You with River!"

In class, a few eyes turn to us.

"Shh, keep it down... it's not official yet. I'm not sure where it's going, but... we clearly like each other! I can hardly believe it!"

"Totally! So, you're going to the game?"

"Yep! I want to see our creations worn, and in action! And I want to support him too..."

The school day passes in a kind of happy haze for me. Every moment spent in class, I find myself daydreaming, thinking back to moments shared with River, anticipating those to come. Even the toughest subjects seem lighter, as if, armed with this new relationship, I'm able to face any challenge. Classes seem like a flick of the wrist to me now. I don't even care about the way other people look at me. It's as if I've just turned a corner. The people at the sewing club won't believe their ears when I tell them all about it.

The hours pass and, surprisingly, I manage to concentrate just enough to participate and take notes, but as soon as the bell rings, my thoughts fly back to River. Julia's encouragement and teasing throughout the day only add to my happiness, making me realize how lucky I am to have a friend like her and someone like River in my life.

When classes finally come to an end, the excitement of the day slowly begins to fade, giving way to a gentle anticipation for the evening. Julia, as social and eager for new experiences as ever, tells me she's going to a party organized by some of our classmates.

"You should come with me, Ava! It would do you good to relax a bit," she enthusiastically suggests.

"Thanks, but I think I'll stay in. I... need some time to myself, to settle down a bit," I retort, a tired smile on my lips.

She seems to understand, and nods with an understanding smile.

"Okay, no problem. But you'll let me know if anything happens with River, won't you?" she insists before leaving.

"No worries! What kind of party is it?"

"Oh, well, you know, it's going to be a rager!"

I frown, then, immediately, she snaps back:

"Well... er... there'll be a good atmosphere."

I hold my gaze, then she yields:

"Well, OK, it's pizza and Netflix night with Mark and Grace. In fact, I'll take them the stuff you bought."

"Oh, I should come and help you!"

I feel guilty leaving them to fend for themselves, knowing on top of that that my poor material management has cost us precious hours.

"Easy, girl! Don't worry about a thing! We'll do just fine. It won't take long now that we've got everything. You know, Mark's a real expert for that sort of sewing! You take it easy!"

I nod reassured that she won't hold a grudge against me. Then she's right. When it comes to sewing and decorating, Mark really is the best!

Alone in our room, I make myself comfortable, determined to spend the evening relaxing. I take out my laptop and log on to my favorite online game. Finally, some peace and quiet after all that. There's nothing like a good role-playing game to take your mind off things.

However, even in the midst of epic battles and sharp dialogue, my mind inevitably drifts back to River. The way he looked at me, his words, his gestures... It all warms my heart and excites me for the future. Despite Julia's absence and the quiet of the room, I don't feel alone. On the contrary, I feel full, sustained by the affection and attention of someone who is beginning to mean a great deal to me.

I check Instagram, to see if I have a message from him and... bingo!

* **River:** *I miss you already*

Oh, boy, is he cute.

* **Ava:** *I miss you too*

Finally, I decide to turn off my computer and crawl under the covers with a smile on my face. It's been a long, emotional day, but I'm feeling amazing. As I close my eyes, I can't wait to see what the future holds. On the other hand, a part of me can't stop worrying. There's the look in other people's eyes. Even though River has told me not to worry about it, there's always Bethany, and I know that if we're really displayed as a couple, she's going to rub it in my face. So, inevitably, the anticipation of this game is both... exhilarating and nerve-wracking.

A week has passed since that night at the motel, and the campus is now buzzing with rumors and whispers about River and I's new relationship. I feel like, for once, the spotlight is on me. Me, who's usually... so shy. Normally, no one is interested in my little person, and suddenly I'm thrust into the spotlight. Despite the generally positive reactions, there's one girl - who, along with her friends, gives me the stink eye when I walk through the corridors.

River and I tried to stay focused on our classes, our friends, and of course, finishing mending jerseys and preparing for his big game. Despite the heightened attention, we managed to find moments just for us, bubbles of tranquility in the whirl-wind of our everyday university life. These shared moments reinforced my belief that, whatever the challenges, we could face them together.

But we're still not together. Not *officially*, anyway.

And now the day of the game has arrived.

I head for the changing rooms, my heart pounding with excitement and a hint of nervousness. As I push open the door, I'm greeted by an electric atmosphere, a mixture of adren-alin and concentration. River, already in his uniform, detaches himself from the group and comes towards me, a big smile on his face.

"Carrot! You've done a fantastic job!" he exclaims, pulling

me into his arms for a brief but tender hug.

"Is everything going the way you want it?" I ask, stepping back to look at him.

"It's perfect! And with you in the stands, it's even better!" His eyes sparkle with infectious confidence.

I give him a friendly pat on the shoulder, a gesture that seems to have become our ritual. Then I turn to the other team members, who greet me with smiles and high-fives. It's clear that, despite my initial fears, I'm accepted here, appreciated even. My apprehension about how others might react fades, replaced by a feeling of belonging.

They thank me warmly for the work done by the sewing club, and I'm pleasantly surprised by the result before my eyes. The fabric additions blend perfectly with the main fabric of the shirts. It gives them a modern, original look, while respecting the primary role of their uniforms: to keep the players mobile without being hindered. It was a long and stressful job, but the result is well worth it!

"Good luck, guys!" I say enthusiastically.

"Thank you, Ava!" they reply in unison, before concentrating again on the coach's final instructions.

River gives me one last look, full of gratitude and affection, before joining his teammates. I discreetly leave, and let the team prepare in the intimacy of their cohesion.

And as they leave the locker room, Coach Harrison comes to find me. Still looking like an old military man. He puts his hands on his hips, then looks me up and down.

"Well, cadet! Looks like you've found more than just jerseys to mend, eh?"

"Indeed, coach. I... I had no idea that..."

"Bah! Don't worry! I think it's great. River has rarely been so motivated. It's great to see."

I think I'm blushing. No, actually: I'm sure I am. I must be peony right now!

"Don't you dare break his heart," resumes the coach with a more serious air. "I need my star in top shape."

To break his heart, he'd have to belong to me. And I'm still not sure.

We haven't said anything to each other. It's like it's a... I don't know... an unspoken agreement? But I'd like to hear it, I'd like to show myself to him a bit more and have him say in front of the others that, yes: I'm his girlfriend.

"I'll do my best..." I say hesitantly.

"Anyway, thanks for all your hard work. You've done a great job! Your reputation will take care of itself with a result like this. But I'll hold up my end of the bargain. Let's go! Get in the stands!"

I obey the coach as if he is my first sergeant and find my place in the stands, my heart swelling with pride. Julia, Grace, and Mark are there too, and they greet me with smiles. I'm grateful to them for coming with me because I know this isn't their sport either. But they were keen to see the result of our sleepless nights.

Julia was admittedly too curious and excited to see sweaty athletes on the ice, and I suspect Grace had the same fantasies, although she'd never admit it. As for Mark, he stressed that it was for a purely professional aspect: admiring his work and making sure nothing went wrong. But of course... I bet he's got a sewing kit with him to run off to the locker room at half-time just in case.

The game starts, and I lose myself in the excitement, en-couraged by the vibrant energy of the rink.

Right from the start of the game, I am captivated by the intensity of the action on the ice. River, as captain, stands out not only for his dexterity and skill with the puck, but also for his natural leadership. I see him directing his teammates with confidence. He communicates nonverbally, using only a glance or a gesture to coordinate their movements. It's incredible to see him so focused and determined.

But clearly, I'm not the only one enjoying the show. Bethany and the other cheerleaders are there, too, a little lower down in the stands. They're cheering on River's team. I don't like seeing her here at all. I have a feeling, things could get out of hand. Especially since the little pest has spotted me. She keeps staring at me, chewing her gum and looking disgusted.

"Ignore her," says Julia, who must sense my discomfort.

Easier said than done... But I try not to glance at her anymore.

At one point, the opposing team launches a rapid offensive. They try to break through our team's defense. River, with almost supernatural anticipation, intercepts the pass, launches a counterattack and, with a precise shot, sends the puck into the opposing net. The ovation from the crowd is deafening, and I can't help but stand up, shouting and applauding with unbridled enthusiasm. It's more than just a game to me now; it's a manifestation of River's passion, dedication and excellence, qualities I deeply admire. I never thought I'd have so much fun watching a hockey game. I mean, e-sport, sure, but here... it still fascinates me, strangely enough. But in the end, I think I'm more interested in the captain than the game.

But what impresses me most is his interaction with his teammates. After every outstanding action, whether his or one of theirs, River is the first to congratulate, encourage and motivate. There's a real camaraderie between them, reinforced by mutual respect and admiration, and I understand that River plays a central role in this dynamic. His leadership is based not only on his individual performances, but also on his ability to bind his team together and get the best out of them.

During a break in the game, as the players gather around

the coach to discuss strategy, I notice River glancing around the stands, searching for someone with his eyes. My heart skips a beat when he meets mine, and a knowing smile lights up his face before he turns back to concentrating on the game. This fleeting exchange fills me with indescribable warmth. In the end, the only one on the sidelines in this team is Peter. I hear he's the one who's been trashing the jerseys, so... he can't be all that nice. But since he brings the water bottles and the players seem grateful, I deduce that he's a nice guy, even if he doesn't seem as tough as the others. Perhaps a gentler nature?

River sends me a kiss from a distance.

I think I'm really falling in love.

As the game progresses, I am amazed by the determination and passion that River and his team put into every second of the game. Winning or losing seems secondary to their team spirit, their desire to go the extra mile for each other. And as the game ends in a well-deserved victory, I realize that my pride in River goes far beyond hockey. It's a standing ovation for the triumphant team.

"It was intense!" exclaims Grace. "I never thought I'd get so caught up in the game."

"You bet! I loved it too," adds Julia.

Mark is just as excited.

"Let's celebrate over a drink," he suggests.

"I'll... I'll... I'll just."

"Yes, we get it, Ava. You go and congratulate the captain."

My friends give me a knowing wink and split the crowd that's starting to rise with the promise that I'll find them later. And that I'll tell them all about it, of course.

It's precisely as they're walking away that Bethany chooses to break the mood.

"I think you're pretty happy for a second-rate geek."

"Bethany? I... I..."

Her girlfriends around her, following in packs, laugh mockingly. In no time at all, I realize that my place in the stands has become an arena, and that the game, even if it's finished on the ice, starts here again. The gossip, the clashes, the highlights, that's what people love. When there's tackling and futility. Inevitably, all eyes turn to me. They want to know how I'm going to react.

But the words just won't come. Every time I look at her: tall, blonde, beautiful, I see her making my life miserable in the locker room and my throat closes up.

"Cat got your tongue, bitch? You look like you're gonna cry now."

"Please, leave me alone."

She mimics me in a mincing voice.

"You're pathetic, my poor girl. Is this how you defend yourself? Look at him, okay?" she says, pointing at River. "Did you get a good look at him?"

I don't answer anything, but she starts again:

"Now look at you. Really look. Look at the way you're dressed, look at your face, and try to understand."

Her every word is cruel beyond compare. I search desperately for River's gaze, but I can't find it. He's still with his teammates, celebrating victory.

"Got it? That's not a gap between you, sweetheart, that's the Grand Canyon. You know what I'm saying? You're no match for River. It's like if Macdonald's thinks it's a Michelin-starred restaurant. So, get the hell out, okay? Everyone thinks it's ridiculous, your little story."

I stammer a few words that choke in my throat.

"I don't understand a word you're saying, either. You're not even together. If he hasn't made you official yet, don't you think there's a reason? You're just the next girl in his fuck list. Nothing more. Then again, he could have chosen better. A passing fancy. A grain of sand. So now, do me a favor, go get a makeover and get out."

With a heavy heart and cheeks burning with humiliation, I quickly turn away, unable to bear another second of this confrontation with Bethany. Her words, sharp and scornful, resonate in my head like a cruel echo. I run away from this crowd, which seems to revel in my distress, to a thunder of laughter.

I run through the campus alleys, tears blurring my vision. I search desperately for a refuge where I can hide, recover from this affront. The pain of humiliation is a weight on my chest, making every breath painful and jerky. I feel ridiculous, ashamed, reduced to nothing by Bethany's venomous words. How could I have believed, even for a moment, that I could belong to this world of hers, to these people who seem so sure of their place, of their right to be loved and respected? For a moment, I flew through the skies imagining I was important to River, but I have to come back to reality: I'm just another girl who dreamed a little too hard.

Without even consciously thinking about it, my steps lead me to the one place where I've always felt accepted, where I can be me without fear of judgment: the sewing club. It's there, among the rolls of fabric, the scattered patterns and the gentle hum of the sewing machines, that I've always found a kind of peace. I'm hoping for a repeat of that feeling tonight.

I hastily unlock the club door and step inside, breathing a sigh of relief. The familiarity of this space envelops me. Here, I'm not mocked or scorned. I'm in my own world.

I collapse into one of the chairs, finally letting the tears flow freely. The silence of the club, usually so comforting, now seems amplified by the tumult of my emotions. I'm crying not only because of Bethany's cruelty, but also for that part of me that had hoped and believed things could be different. How stupid I was. How naive I've been...

Bethany hit the nail on the head.

It's only a few minutes before the door opens softly, and I look up, expecting to see one of the club members. But it's not a familiar face from sewing club that appears; it's River. His expression quickly changes from concern to pain when he sees me like this, collapsed and vulnerable.

"Ava," he mutters, approaching cautiously, as if afraid that one more step might break me further.

I want to tell him to go away, that I don't want to see anyone, but the sight of him, here to find me, warms my heart in spite of myself. River kneels before me, gently wiping a tear from my cheek with his thumb.

"I don't want to talk," I sniffle.

"I heard what happened with Bethany. She was a jerk."

Jerk is not the word. Cruel would be more appropriate.

"Everyone laughed. They agree with her. Is that what you think too?"

"Of course not. Don't listen to her, Bethany doesn't know what she's talking about. She's just... jealous," he says softly.

Jealous? The idea seems so absurd that, despite the sadness, a stifled laugh escapes my lips.

"Jealous? Of me? But look at me, River. I... How could she envy me?"

River takes my hands in his, forcing me to look at him.

"Because you're amazing, Ava. You're kind, smart, passionate and beautiful... You have a huge heart, and you see the world in a way that no one else can. Bethany could never understand what it's like to be truly loved for who she is. But I do."

His words are a balm to my battered soul. For the first time since I entered this room, I feel a little less lost, a little less alone. River gently pulls me to my feet, wrapping me in his arms. His embrace is firm, protective, and for the first time all day, I feel safe. Bethany has managed to spoil all my joy at the game.

"I loved watching you play," I whisper.

"And I loved having you here. You don't have to hide here, Carrot. It doesn't matter what other people say or think."

The sincerity in his voice, the warmth of his embrace, finally allows me to breathe. Maybe, in the face of adversity, doubt and cruelty, having someone like River by my side is all I need to be strong.

Before I know it, he's kissing me passionately. I wasn't ready for it, but it feels good, nonetheless. I get the feeling that he's trying to make up for my pain by being present, and it works very well.

"Thank you for coming."

"Thank you for inviting me," I retort, recovering his lips against mine.

What is it with me, every time I'm near him? It's like I forget my tears. Every time, he gives me the courage to go ahead and try crazier and crazier things, and... this time, it's me who wants him deeply. I decide to take the lead. I can't always let him make the first move.

"What are you..."

"Shhhh," I say, slowly undressing him.

"Ava, but... we're in the sewing club, and..."

"And I know no one will come. I'm telling you."

My answer seems to suit him, and without paying any more attention to his last worries, River lets himself go to my caresses.

For once, I have sincere and shared feelings.

For once, I can experience something a little exhilarating. A little exciting, in my life, I don't want to miss out. I want to sink my teeth into this passion, even if it burns me in the process. I'd be a fool not to give it a try.

And since we don't have protection, we have to find more creative - but still very enjoyable - ways. Especially as River is particularly dexterous with his fingers. Every time he inserts them inside me, I moan and sigh as if my whole body is about to give out. He gives me so much that I don't think I'll be able to give him back every hundredth time. Yet he seems satisfied, too.

We sleep together. We flirt. But where are we really? Because behind all the laughing and sighing and moaning, nothing else is going on. And... if I'm being perfectly honest, River's reputation terrifies me. I know what the others expect of him: to parade around with a charismatic girl on his arm. Not a geek like me. What he really needs for his image is a girl like Bethany. But I don't feel she knows him like I do.

Breathless and sweaty, we put our clothes back on after each of us had experienced ecstasy.

"River, I..."

"Yes?"

"I was wondering where we stand, you and I."

"Why do you ask that, Carrot?"

I have the impression that he doesn't understand that I need to know.

"I'm just wondering how you see other people's opinions of us. I can see that... it's all very discreet."

"We're just flirting. There's nothing wrong with that. Is there?"

That's all there is to it.

Flirting?

Nothing but flirting!

I can imagine what River was like before. Given his passion for science and everything else, I'm pretty sure he didn't exactly belong to the cool club before he went to university. But he's given himself a new image. He's probably suffered, and

144

he doesn't want to go back. He doesn't want to go through what I'm going through. The daily harassment, the others who look at you sideways because you have unusual passions... That's my life, but him... If he displays himself with me, then he knows he'll fall back into that kind of image and that's not what he wants. I feel he's torn, but it'll never go any further. Not the way I imagine it, anyway. Not by making a statement under my bedroom window, guitar in hand. Not by telling everyone that, yes, I'm his girlfriend. Not by kissing me full on the mouth in the middle of campus. I'm not a secret, but I'm not official either. I have to make up my mind. He's not going to give up his image and his career for a girl as insipid as me, hiding behind her mane and big glasses.

Just as these thoughts cloud my mind, River's phone rings, cutting through the heavy silence between us. He glances at the screen before picking up, his expression immediately transformed into a neutral wall.

"Yeah?" he says, his voice devoid of the emotion that colored our exchanges a few minutes ago.

I watch him, trying to discern behind his mask the nature of the conversation, but he pulls away slightly, as if to keep me out of this exchange.

"No, I'm not doing anything special," he finally replies after listening carefully. "I'll be there in a minute."

He hangs up and looks at me. His eyes search mine. There's a moment of silence, a suspended moment when everything that hasn't been said seems to float between us.

"It was the guys from the team," he explains, without my having to ask. "They were wondering where I'd been."

I nod, trying to mask my disappointment. 'Nothing special,' these words resonate within me with a bitterness I didn't expect.

"You have to go," I mutter, forcing myself to smile.

145

"Ava," he begins, hesitantly.

His hand rises as if to touch my face, but he holds back at the last moment.

"I... I don't want you to think..."

"It's okay, River. I understand," I cut him off.

I don't want to hear him say something that could hurt more. Not a lame apology, anyway.

"Go back to your team. They're counting on you."

He looks at me a moment longer, his gaze full of unspoken things, then nods softly. Without another word, he gets up and heads for the door, glancing back one last time before leaving. He leaves me alone with my thoughts and the weight of my reality.

The door closes behind him with a faint click, and I suddenly feel very alone. Bethany's words, River's departure, all weigh heavily on my shoulders. I gather my things in a mechanical gesture, my thoughts still clouded by the day's events. The solitude of the sewing club, once a refuge, now seems too vast, too silent.

Why does it hurt so much?

11

The next morning, I wake up with a weight on my heart, a heaviness that seems to have infused my dreams. I didn't even play on the computer; I was so sad yesterday. It was awful. What was supposed to be a great day turned out to be... horrible! I lay staring at the ceiling, trying to summon the strength to face the day. But every thought of River, of Bethany, of yesterday, only adds to the weight.

When Julia comes out of the bathroom, her face lights up with a smile that quickly fades when she sees me, still in bed when I should already be getting ready.

"Ava, what's wrong? Do you look... unwell? Besides, you didn't say anything about yesterday. Did you get a chance to meet River after the game? We didn't hear from you, so we assumed..."

I try to smile, but it's a pale, lifeless gesture. What's the point of lying? I've been in constant turmoil ever since River and I started dating. It's been a constant up and down. And I've never been a fan of roller coasters!

"I'm... I'm just tired," I say, sitting up.

But Julia doesn't believe me. She sits on the edge of my bed, her eyes full of concern. She knows when I'm lying. She's my best friend for a reason.

"Ava, it's me. Tell me about it. It's River, isn't it? Do I have to sew his balls?!"

The words race to the edge of my lips, but I hesitate. Sharing my pain seems both necessary and insurmountable. Finally, the words escape, and I tell her about the confrontation with Bethany, River's coldness, the feeling of being totally outside my own body, inadequate and unwanted.

Julia listens attentively, her expression shifting from concern to indignation.

"Ava don't let anyone, especially Bethany, make you feel that way. And River... he'd better behave, or he'll have me to deal with. I swear I'll sew his..."

"Balls, yes, I get it..."

She tries to wring a smile from me, and this time I feel a spark of warmth in response. Julia has always had the gift of bringing a little light to my darkest moments. There's her and... the computer for that.

"Thank you, Julia," I mutter, my voice still fragile.

"Come on, get dressed. We're gonna face this day together. And don't worry, I'm here. We'll get you through this. You're the president of the sewing club, aren't you? You're not just anyone, you know!"

"Pfft. You're talking nonsense, but it's funny..."

In class, I try to concentrate on the teacher's words, but my thoughts wander, inevitably drawn back to recent events. Then Peter, whom I only know through his interactions with the hockey team, approaches me at the end of class.

He's a medium-sized boy, neither too tall nor too short, with tousled brown hair that gives him a casual yet studious air. His soft brown eyes reflect a rare kind of warmth and understanding. Unlike the other players on the hockey team, he doesn't look imposing or intimidating; rather, he's the kind of person you can count on, stable and reliable. Although his build resembles that of a sportsman rather than an average student. He wears simple clothes, jeans and a university T-shirt, but it's his open posture and sincere smile that make him instantly likable. He also seems shyer than the others. I have to say, this makes me feel less paralyzed, which is a good thing. After everything I've been through these past few weeks... I could do with a bit more 'normality' in my life.

"Hi, Ava. Um... I just wanted to tell you that I saw what happened yesterday with Bethany," he begins, awkwardly.

I look at him, surprised by his approach. Peter's always been that guy, a bit behind the scenes, less imposing than the other players on the team. But he's also the one who apparently sabotaged the jerseys.

"Oh, uh... Okay..."

"It was really ugly of her. Don't let her hurt you like that. Bethany's... she's just jealous, you know?"

His words take me by surprise. Jealous? Of me?

"Jealous? Of what?"

It's not the first time I've been told that, strangely enough...

Peter seems to be searching for words.

"You and River, I suppose. You look... well, you look good together. And Bethany doesn't like to lose what she considers hers, even if... well, even if River doesn't belong to her."

I stand there speechless, processing the information. Peter, seeing my confusion, quickly adds:

"I just wanted you to know that not everyone thinks like she does. And... uh... if you need anything, I'm here."

I look at him, touched by his gesture. Peter, whom I hardly know, is unexpectedly kind.

"Thank you, Peter. That's really sweet of you, I... it means a lot to me. But you know... River and I... well... it's not as... as simple. We're not... really together."

"Oh. OKAY. I see. Well... Uh... and... I hear you play online games, so... I wanted to leave you my gamertag[5] , if you want

---

5 A *gamertag is* a nickname and avatar that represents the player when

149

to add me?"

He puts a piece of paper in front of me - as a high-school student from the 2000s would have done - with his nickname written on it. It's so unexpected and... kind of cute.

He smiles at me, a little embarrassed, then walks away, leaving me there with a glimmer of hope and the feeling that maybe I'm not as alone as I thought.

Julia brings me back to reality.

"Hey, don't go knocking over every guy on campus, okay? But... I must admit, this one is particularly thoughtful."

As sweet as Peter is, I can't stop thinking about River.

By the time we get back to our room, it's well into the afternoon. Julia sees my lost gaze staring at the computer screen without really seeing it. She gives me a friendly nudge.

"Come on, Ava, add him. It'll take your mind off things," she insists, a mischievous smile on her lips.

I sigh, but part of me knows she's right. It's been a long time since I've played with anyone but Maeline. Maybe sharing a game with Peter will get me out of my own head for a while.

"Okay," I finally relent, opening my gaming app and searching for his gamertag.

Once added, it's not long before I receive an invitation to join a game. With a slightly lighter heart, I launch into the game.

"Come on, show him what you can do! I'm going to do my homework," says Julia.

★ **LordMoon:** *Hi! Ready for a game?*

★ **DarkAngelOfDeath666:** *Yep, definitely. I didn't know you played until you told me earlier.*

★ **LordMoon:** *It's not something I talk about too much. The*

---

playing online games, and can be exchanged to contact other players.

guys on the team would laugh at me, even more than usual. They're not mean, but they can be annoying eh...

Online conversation with Peter is surprisingly easy. He has a subtle sense of humor and a way of looking at things that makes me smile. After a particularly successful maneuver, he even compliments me.

* **LordMoon:** *You play really well!*
* **DarkAngelOfDeath666:** *Thanks, you're not bad yourself.*
* **LordMoon:** *I've had a lot of practice!*
* **DarkAngelOfDeath666:** *You bet! I bet you've played less hours than I have. You're good, really!*

I didn't think a guy who hangs out with the hockey team, like River, could be so likable. I mean... he's a far cry from the stereotypes I had of sportsmen.

One more...

I try not to think about River and shake my head to get back to my game in progress. As our characters fight side by side in the game, Peter throws out an unexpected topic.

* **LordMoon:** *About the torn jerseys... I wanted to tell you it wasn't me. I know everyone thinks that... but... I didn't do anything.*

I'm surprised by his statement. I decide to continue on the subject, intrigued.

* **DarkAngelOfDeath666:** *Really? But everyone thought...*
* **LordMoon:** *I know, and it bothers me. I've been accused because I don't get along with some of the guys on the team, but I would never do something like that.*

★ **DarkAngelOfDeath666:** *But who, then?*
★ **LordMoon:** *I don't know. I really don't. But I've been found guilty. It suits everyone...*
    ★ **DarkAngelOfDeath666:** *You didn't try to set the record straight?*
    ★ **LordMoon:** *I did, but they're fine with it being me, you know...*

I suddenly feel guilty for even indirectly suspecting him.

    ★ **DarkAngelOfDeath666:** *I'm sorry I thought it was you. It's just not fair.*
    ★ **LordMoon:** *Don't worry. I understand why people might think that. But I wanted you to know the truth. By the way, I really appreciate that you took matters into your own hands to repair the jerseys.*

I smile at my screen, touched by his sincerity.

    ★ **DarkAngelOfDeath666:** *Thank you, Peter. The sewing club has never been more in demand!*
    ★ **LordMoon:** *With your talent, it will be again! I've seen the finalized jerseys and it's great work!*

I feel a bond forming, an unexpected but pleasant connection.

    ★ **DarkAngelOfDeath666:** *Thank you!*

I wonder who could have sabotaged the team so badly, if it's not him... But he has no interest in lying to me. Why should he? We hardly know each other.

We continue to play, exchanging strategies and virtual

laughter. When I finally switch off the computer, I don't know why, but I feel a slight relief. It's as if, all of a sudden, I'm understood by someone other than my usual friends.

The next day, after my online conversation with Peter, I feel strangely light-headed on my way to class. Last night, discovering that Peter shared my secret passions added a layer of excitement to my usually predictable routine. Despite Peter's revelation, part of me is still hanging on this intrigue and suspicion surrounding the hockey team. Someone must have sabotaged those jerseys! But who?

As I cross the campus, Julia at my side, my gaze stops on River. There he is, surrounded by his teammates. He radiates that special glow reserved for popular athletes. Yet when our eyes meet, I detect a hesitation, a subtle change in his attitude. He approaches, his usual smile slightly forced, and I brace myself for a cordial exchange.

"How are you?" he asks.

He really has a gift for nonchalance, that one...

"Uh... I'm okay. And... how about you?"

"I'll leave you to it," says Julia.

"No, don't..."

Oh crap, she's already gone!

"It was... it was a great game," I stammer.

I don't know what else to say, damn it! I must look ridiculous!

"Yeah. Too bad for the way things turned out after that..."

That's for sure.

Our exchange is interrupted by Bethany's arrival, which immediately casts a chill. River stiffens, and his attention wanders.

"River, baby, what are you still doing here? We've got class!"

"Don't call me that," he squeaks. "You and I, we... rah, never mind."

But, under pressure from Bethany and the others, River turns away from me. He offers me a final, forced smile before walking away, leaving me alone with my thoughts.

As I continue on my way, I feel torn. On the one hand, Peter, with whom I share so much and who seems so sincere. On the other, River, complex and elusive, who blows hot and cold with disconcerting ease. I don't yet know where all this will lead me, but one thing's for sure: my university life is becoming infinitely more complicated.

At break time, I head for the cafeteria, my thoughts in disarray after my encounter with River and Bethany's interruption. I can't help but feel a little desperate at the thought of Bethany wanting to get back at River. That girl has always had a way of making me feel inferior, and seeing River let himself be influenced by her, even in spite of himself, hurts my heart. It really does.

I meet Julia at our usual table, a touch of anxiety in my stomach.

"Did you see what happened just now?" I exclaim, unable to contain my frustration.

Julia nods, her eyes full of compassion.

"Yes, I saw. Don't let Bethany get you down. You know what she's like."

"I know, but it drives me crazy to see River acting like this... Like he can't assert himself in front of her," I sigh.

My friend grimaces.

"River is complicated, Ava. But that's not who you should focus on. Peter, for example, seems genuinely interested in you. And he's a good guy. What do you think? I don't like seeing you like this... I'd rather you were with a guy who deserves you."

I'm about to answer when Peter approaches our table, a tray in hand.

"Hi, can I sit here?" he asks with a shy smile.

Julia and I exchange a quick glance before nodding.

"Of course," I say, making room for him.

Peter settles in, and the atmosphere lightens. We start talking about anything and everything, carefully avoiding the subject of River and the damaged jerseys.

"That was a great game last night," he exclaims. "You really are a champion!"

I'd almost blush. But then, my little gaming prowess is nothing compared to what he and his team are capable of in sport.

I can see River glaring at me. He doesn't look happy.

Peter's mention of our online game brings a smile to my face. It's strange to feel valued for something so far removed from River's world and sporting exploits.

"Thanks, but I'm not the only one playing," I retort, modestly, while glancing at River on the other side of the cafeteria.

I can't help but notice the intensity of his gaze. He seems almost... disturbed, as if he doesn't appreciate seeing me laughing and chatting so easily with Peter. It's disconcerting to realize that River, despite his apparent disinterest, remains attentive to my interactions. Why should it bother him so much?

"You know, Ava, I really think you're talented. And not just at video games. The sewing club is lucky to have you. You did an amazing job with the jerseys!"

Julia nods in agreement.

"Absolutely. She's a little genius who doesn't know it!"

These words warm my heart, and for a moment I allow myself to forget River and his puzzled looks.

"You give me too much importance, I assure you..."

I want to hide because their compliments make me blush. But at the same time, they seem so sincere...

Yet despite the warmth of this exchange, I feel River's eyes on me. His presence troubles and questions me.

Why now? Why this sudden interest?

I shake my head, trying to banish these thoughts.

"And tonight, Peter, I'm looking forward to beating you again," I say in a light tone.

Peter bursts out laughing.

"We'll see about that. Prepare for a memorable defeat."

The rest of lunch is spent in a relaxed atmosphere, punctuated by laughter and friendly teasing. But deep down, I'm still aware of River's glances, this unwanted attention that sows doubt in my mind. What does it mean? Is it jealousy, curiosity, or something even more complicated?

I decide to put these questions aside for the time being. Besides, it's not just River looking at me. There's also Bethany, sitting right next to him. She's talking to him, but he doesn't seem the least bit interested. He only has eyes for the table I'm sharing with Julia and Peter.

It's too weird, this situation. Too weird...

Shortly after dinner and the promise of a memorable evening in Peter's company - on the game, anyway - I head off to the sewing club to collect the rest of the jerseys that weren't used in their last game, to take to the hockey club. This way, I think I've definitely marked the end of my collaboration with River, and perhaps this gesture will allow me to mourn the loss of all that.

Just as I'm about to go through the changing room door, I hear screams and stop dead in my tracks.

I stand still, listening, my heart racing. Bethany's voice, sharp and cutting, pierces the silence of the corridor.

"Why do you spend so much time with that... girl?" she spits.

Her anger is palpable even through the closed door.

"You're much too considerate, much too nice to her! She

doesn't deserve it. She's a fucking nerd!"

There's a pause, then comes River's voice, calmer, but with a hint of frustration.

"Bethany, stop. It's not what you think."

"Is that right? And what am I supposed to think, River? That you've suddenly found an interest in sewing? I think it's that little idiot you're interested in."

Jealousy oozes from every word.

"It's not that," retorts River. "Ava has helped the team, and it's only natural that I should be... grateful."

"Grateful?" exclaims Bethany, as her voice goes up a notch. "You've never been 'grateful' like that with me. What's so special about her, eh?"

I feel petrified as I listen to their argument, which seems to reveal far more about River's feelings than I ever dared to imagine. My heart sinks at the thought of him defending our relationship, even if it's to Bethany. He keeps up the mask for others, but in private, he doesn't hesitate to take my side.

Well, even if what he's saying isn't exactly pleasant to hear.

"She's different," River finally says. "And it doesn't concern you, Bethany. What happened between us is over."

"Anyway, it's over with her, isn't it? You saw how close Peter got to her, didn't you?"

"Don't talk about that. You're talking nonsense!"

"Ah, so it bothers you?"

Bethany presses him, clearly trying to provoke him.

"I thought you didn't care about Ava. But maybe I'm wrong... Maybe the great River is jealous?" she insists, stepping into the breach.

There's a pause, during which I can almost imagine River weighing his words carefully.

"How I feel or don't feel about Ava is none of your business, Bethany. And it's not about jealousy. It's just... it's not

157

fair to drag her into our stories."

"You should really let her go."

"Oh yes, and why?"

"Because she's fucking dragging you down! Can't you see that everyone thinks she's weird?"

"You're talking nonsense, Bethany. The team likes her."

"And it's just plain weird! Nobody's interested in her. Think of your reputation. Damn it, River, I'm sick of this crap!"

A heavy silence ensues, cut only by the muffled sound of furious footsteps. Bethany must have left the lockers because the door swings open. I step back just in time to avoid being seen. My heart is pounding.

River comes out a few moments later. He seems lost in thought. He doesn't see me, and I remain hidden, trying to process the information I've heard. River's defense touches me deeply, and at the same time, it confuses me. Why should he feel obliged to defend me? And above all, why does it make me feel such a complex mix of emotions?

I take a deep breath and decide to leave these thoughts for later. For now, I need to concentrate on the task in hand: finishing what I've started with the jerseys. I set them down carefully, then, as I make my way towards the sewing club premises, River's words echo in my head. They stay with me like the echo of an unspoken promise. This unexpected confrontation between River and Bethany changes something in me. It rekindles hopes I had tried to suppress. But for now, I have to keep a cool head and concentrate on the present, even if the future suddenly seems a lot less certain.

12

Is it possible to expect such a brutal descent into hell? In the morning, after a good night of video games with Peter, I reach for my phone to check my social networks.

"Wait, uh... Ava, you shouldn't..." Julia tells me.

I frown, suddenly suspicious.

"What? What's going on?"

"Nothing much, really, but there's something we need to talk about. Briefly. I just... I just want to check something out, okay?"

The concern in Julia's voice immediately catches my attention, and I pause the opening of my apps.

"You're starting to worry me. What's going on?"

My voice trembles slightly.

Julia takes a deep breath, and I can see she's weighing her words carefully.

"It's just... There are rumors circulating on social networks. About hockey team jerseys."

She pauses, scrutinizing my reaction.

I can feel my heart speeding up.

"What rumors?"

I'm not sure I want to hear the answer.

"They say that... that it was you who damaged the jerseys to get closer to River."

Instantly, my stomach knots.

159

"What? But it's completely false! Why would anyone say that?"

Julia gently places her hand on mine. She hands me a coffee - as usual.

"I know Ava. I know it's not true. But you know how people are... One little spark and everything goes up in flames. Especially with social networks."

I quickly unlock my phone, my heart beating wildly. Notifications pile up, and I see mentions, shares, and even hashtags related to the #PickMeGirl[6] rumor. My name is everywhere, accompanied by accusatory and mocking comments. It's like the ground is shifting beneath my feet.

"I... I don't know what to do. Who could have invented such a thing?" I mutter.

"I don't know about that. But we'll deal with it. We'll find a way to set the record straight."

Armed with a fragile determination, I try to make my way through the university corridors, each step costing me more than the last. Furtive glances and thinly veiled whispers follow me, like mocking ghosts. I can almost hear their thoughts, the silent accusations weighing on my shoulders. It's a horrible situation. Once again, I'm in the spotlight, but this time I have a disastrous reputation. I just wish someone would come to my defense. To be helped. But the only sympathetic messages came from the sewing club.

"Did you see that? It's her, the girl who sabotaged the jerseys," whispers a voice as I pass.

"She must be desperate to get his attention," sneers another.

I grit my teeth as I focus on the ground in front of me, hoping that if I don't look at them, I'll be able to imagine myself

---

6 Hashtag used in particular to designate a girl who wants to be chosen at all costs and make herself look good.

somewhere else, far away from this nightmare. But as I turn a corner, I find myself face to face with Bethany and her pack, as if fate has decided to test me even further.

"Oh, look who's here! The sabotaging seamstress. Have you lost your way? Or are you still trying to get closer to River by any means necessary?"

Her cruel smile leaves no escape.

Her group laughs and their venomous echoes hit me hard. I suddenly feel small, vulnerable, but I refuse to give them the satisfaction of seeing me broken. It's not acceptable!

"You have officially become the most pathetic girl on campus. Can you believe it? You're finally the first one somewhere. You must be happy, right?"

"What you say is wrong."

My voice is firmer than I thought possible, carried by a wave of unsuspected courage.

Her surprise is short-lived, quickly replaced by renewed contempt.

"Oh, really? And who's going to believe you? Stop showing your claws and thinking you're a tiger, because you're pathetic. You're a kitten. That's all you are. And then again... kittens are kind of cute and you... We'd like to ask you, why you don't comb your hair a bit?"

She glares at me, sure of her victory in this cruel game of popularity.

In this world where appearances reign supreme, my word seems paltry compared to theirs. I can't win this fight anyway.

"Hey, you three," says Peter, coming up to my level. "Leave her alone, will you?"

"Here's the knight in shining armor," Bethany teases. "Don't worry. Here you have your princess."

"Don't listen to them, Ava, they're stupid."

I walk away with a heavy heart, leaving the laughter and

mockery behind me. The day stretches on in a succession of painful moments. All I want to do is disappear. In class, I receive a pile of papers in my face, subtle mockery slipped into the corridors and... the hashtags about me go on and on. It's unbearable.

The day is finally coming to an end. Just as well, I want to curl up in bed and never get out again. Just as I'm getting ready to find some semblance of peace on my computer or by merging with my pillow, my phone vibrates. It's a message from River.

⋆ **River:** *Can we meet after school?*

My heart stops for a moment. After everything that's happened, after all these rumors, what could he possibly want to tell me? He doesn't even ask me how I'm doing... Nothing, not even a 'hello'.
Not good. Not good at all.

⋆ **Ava:** *Okay*
⋆ **River:** *Meet me at 5:30 p.m., hockey club*

With growing apprehension, I head for the meeting place. My legs seem to have turned to lead. I feel like turning back at any moment.

River is already there, his face marked by an unusual magnitude.

"Ava, you came, I... I need to ask you something."

I nod, although my hands are shaking slightly. I know exactly what he's going to say, and it hurts just thinking about it. But I have to stay strong. I've got no choice. I have to face this.

"I'm listening."

He takes a deep breath, his eyes locked on mine.

"Did you sabotage the jerseys?"

His voice is tinged with a doubt that pierces my heart. I'm stunned.

"No, River, of course not! Why would I do such a thing?"

I feel like crying. I'm going to burst into tears. I can't see any other way.

Because he's there, in front of me, and I can see that he's having doubts. After all the moments I've spent with him, after he was my first time... He still doubts. I've given him everything I hold most precious and he... he doesn't trust me.

River looks away. He seems to be wrestling with his own thoughts.

"I... I don't know. Everyone's talking about it, and Bethany..."

"And you believe Bethany? You know me, River. You know I would never do something like that."

He looks at me again, his eyes filled with inner conflict.

"I want to believe you, Ava, I really do. But it's complicated. Everything is so complicated right now. It's the team, too, you know... they think that... that it's possible."

The ensuing silence is heavy, laden with a mixture of unspoken emotions. Finally, River adds:

"I'm sorry. I don't know what to think."

I feel devastated, betrayed by the doubt of the man for whom I had begun to have strong feelings.

"If you don't believe me, then I don't know why I'm here," I whisper in a shaken voice.

Without waiting for his answer, I turn and walk away, tears blurring my vision. The trust and friendship I'd hoped was still possible with River seems to be fading, giving way to deep loneliness and despair. I have real feelings for him. That's the worst of it. It's so painful. So unfair. Maybe that's what hurts the most, in the end. The pain caused by this damned injustice.

When I get to my room, I can hardly breathe. I'm still stunned by this day, it was so shitty, it deserves its place in the annals of the worst days ever.

"So er... do you want to talk about it, or...?" asks Julia when she sees my face.

"I want to disappear. Do you understand that? The whole campus is throwing up on me, and I didn't do anything."

I let myself fall against the door, still unable to contain my tears. The pressure of the day is pouring down my cheeks.

"Sweetie, I'm... I'm so sorry for you. I don't know who could have started such a rumor, but I want you to know that no one at the sewing club believes any of it."

Julia approaches and takes me in her arms. She holds me close. Her presence is a small comfort in the whirlwind of my emotions.

"Thank you," I murmur, my voice choked with sobs.

★ ★ ★

The next morning, Julia stands in front of my bed. She's still waiting for me, but I've decided not to move.

"Ava, you really should come to class today. It'll only make things worse if you hide."

I shake my head, wrapped in my blanket like a protective shell.

"I can't, Julia. I couldn't bear their looks, their whispers... I'd rather stay here."

"I understand," she sighs, "but you're not alone, okay? Don't let them win... You're better than that."

I offer her a weak smile in thanks, but as soon as she leaves the room, I turn to my computer. Today, I'd rather fight dragons and explore dungeons than face the reality of my campus. Dragons seem far less terrifying than Bethany.

As I lose myself in these fictional universes, I find a semblance of peace. Every quest I complete, every level I pass, gives me the illusion of controlling at least part of my life. Peter joins me online after a few hours. He brings with him a welcome distraction and news from outside.

★ **LordMoon:** *How are you feeling?*
★ **DarkAngelOfDeath666** : *A little better, now that I'm here*
★ **LordMoon:** *Good*
★ **DarkAngelOfDeath666:** *It wasn't too... terrible today?*
★ **LordMoon:** It's *best if you don't look at your phone.*

The day passes in a bubble of pretend normalcy, but reality catches up with me every time I take a break. The notifications on my phone, the unread messages, the declined invitations... I know I can't run forever.

I don't know what to think anymore.

I don't really want to know.

Dusk tints my room with a soft orange light as I hear the door open. Julia enters, a look of compassion and concern on her face. She sits beside me on the bed with a grave expression.

"River was looking for you today at noon. He wanted to talk to you," she says.

I raise my head, intrigued in spite of myself. The mere mention of his name makes my pulse beat a little faster.

"Really?"

"Yes. He seemed... different. I don't know exactly what he wanted, but I think he's sorry he didn't believe you," she explains gently.

I'm perplexed by the news, part of me wanting to believe in a possible change, the other fearing that I'll be disappointed again.

"So what? What am I supposed to do with this?" I ask, my

voice tinged with fatigue.

"Maybe give him a chance to explain himself?"

Julia asks cautiously. She knows she's walking on eggshells.

"I know this has been very hard for you, Ava. But if River has made the effort to seek you out, maybe he's worth listening to."

I sigh - because I feel torn.

"I don't know, Julia. After everything that's happened, I'm not sure I can just... forgive and forget."

"No one's asking you to forget, Ava. But maybe forgiving, or at least listening to what he has to say, could help you. Help both of you. Move on."

She squeezes my hand in hers and it reminds me of when she used to take care of me when we were in high school. We've always been close.

I look at her, searching in her eyes for a sureness, I'm struggling to find in myself. Finally, I nod gently.

"I'll... I'll talk to him. See what he has to say."

Julia smiles warmly at me.

"That's my warrior! I think it's the right thing to do. And who knows? It might clear up a lot of things."

My hands are practically shaking as I reach for my phone to send him a message on Instagram.

I'm afraid...

⋆ **Ava:** *Hi, River. Julia said you wanted to talk?*

River's reply comes quickly, almost as if he'd been waiting impatiently for my message.

⋆ **River:** *Yes, I think we really need to talk. Can you meet me in the campus park in an hour?*

I read and reread his message, my heart beating wildly. It's as if every word adds both weight and hope to my shoulders. I type a quick reply, telling him I'll be there, before dropping back on my bed, staring at the ceiling.

"Are you all right?" Julia asks with concern.

"Yes. See you in an hour at the park," I murmur.

"Do you want me to come with you?"

I shake my head.

"No, I have to do this alone. Thanks, though."

"You want me to lend you a condom..."

"No, I mean it, Julia. I won't be needing it now."

"You never know... a dirty rendezvous in the park!"

"Stop... I just want to explain to River. I want to understand what happened."

An hour later, I head for the park and every step echoes my heartbeat. The place is quiet, with just the rustle of leaves and distant birdsong to keep me company.

River is already there, sitting on a bench, lost in thought. He stands up as soon as he sees me, a mixture of apprehension and relief in his eyes.

"You came."

I stand at a cautious distance, unsure of what's coming next. Fuck, I feel so bad. I've got to get my confidence back. I take a deep breath, but it's no use. I'm practically speechless.

"You wanted to talk, so let's talk."

River takes a deep breath in turn.

"I'm... I'm sorry. I'm sorry for everything. I should never have doubted you or put you in that position."

"What happened to make you change your mind?"

River looks down slightly.

"I talked to Peter, that's all. He told me it wasn't him. Besides... I knew, really. The thing is, it's my fault. And nobody else's. I shouldn't have left the door open. I'm not looking for someone to blame, okay? But... I know it's not you."

His words hit me right in the heart, a mixture of relief and sadness washing over me.

"Why now? Why change your mind?"

"Well, you know... Peter can be pretty convincing when he wants to be. When he thought I'd blamed you, he almost hit me. And I realized I'd been a fool. Blaming you, judging you without knowing the whole story. I... I want you to know that I believe you. And I want to help you clear your name if you'll let me."

"Wait... Peter tried to hit you?"

"Yeah," he laughs. "Funny, isn't it? I figured if a twig like him was brave enough to defend your honor in front of the rest of the team, I was really a coward for not doing it too. I was a jerk, I'm sorry."

There's sincerity in his eyes that I hadn't seen before, a vulnerability that makes me waver.

"River, I... I don't know what to say."

"Just tell me you're willing to let me try to fix my mistakes. That you're willing to let me be there for you, like I should have been from the start."

We stand there in a charged silence, and the world seems to hold its breath around us.

Finally, I find my voice, still trembling, but buoyed by a budding glimmer of hope.

"Okay, River. We'll try to fix it."

His face lights up with a smile, and for the first time in a long time, I feel a weight lifted from my shoulders. River moves a little closer, his gesture symbolically narrowing the space created by misunderstandings and doubts.

He grabs my hands and my heart races.

"Thank you, Ava. I'm going to talk to the team, to everyone

who heard the rumor. I'll make sure they know the truth. That it was my fault, and that you had nothing to do with it."

"You're... you're going to sacrifice your reputation?"

He shrugs and smiles.

"I'm not sacrificing anything. I'm telling the truth. I think that's the most important thing, don't you?"

I don't know what to say. Usually, people like River - who are popular, anyway - are always protecting appearances where they're concerned. But this time, I feel like all that's disappearing and he's willing to let the truth come out.

"What about Bethany?" I ask, a hint of concern in my voice.

River grimaces slightly.

"Bethany... it's gonna be complicated. But I'll talk to her too. She needs to understand that her actions have consequences. I'll take care of it, I promise."

I nod, grateful, but still a little skeptical about the outcome of the conversations to come. Still, River's determination gives me hope. Perhaps, in the end, this story will find a happy ending, or at least, a little fairer as far as I'm concerned. Because, frankly, I've really had it.

"What about Peter? He deserves a big thank you, I suppose," I say with a half-smile.

River is still holding my hands.

"Absolutely," River agrees with a laugh. "I owe him a beer, at the very least. He was amazing. He almost took a beating from more than one of the guys on the team when he called me out, but hey, I don't think he cared. You seem to mean a lot to him..."

The sun begins to set, painting the sky in warm colors. River and I continue to talk, no longer as two people in conflict, but as two friends trying to rebuild what has been damaged.

"What... what do you mean?" I ask.

"What I mean is... if you prefer Peter, I'd understand," he

lets out in an almost inaudible whisper. "He's... he's a nice guy, frankly, and I can see how you might like him. I don't want to get between..."

I shake my head, interrupting his flow of words.

"River, that's not the case. Peter is... really a very nice boy, and an online playmate, now. But that's about it. The way I feel about him... it's not what you think."

And it couldn't be truer. Because it's every time I get close to River that my heart beats a thousand miles an hour.

Peter's nice, but it's not the same thing.

River looks at me, and I think he's searching my eyes for the sincerity of my words. Slowly, he seems to find the answers to his unasked questions. He lets out a sigh of relief.

"I'm glad to hear it," he admits with a shy smile. "I just wanted to be sure. Because, you know, after everything that's happened, I realize how stupid I've been. How I put our... what we had in jeopardy, for no good reason."

The sun finishes its course, leaving behind a soft light that envelops the park in a serene atmosphere. We sit for a while in this calm, enjoying the tranquility of twilight.

"You know, River, what matters to me is truth and sincerity," I say at last, breaking the silence. "And I'm glad you chose to do the right thing, not just for me, but for yourself too."

"I'm doing it because it's important. And because I care about you, Ava. More than I realized," he admits with a tender look.

We rise from the bench. Our shadows stretch on the way home. As we walk side by side, I feel a weight lift from my shoulders. The challenges ahead seem less daunting with River by my side, ready to face rumors and misunderstandings with me.

The journey back to my room is made in comfortable silence, punctuated only by our footsteps on the campus path.

The night is mild, and the fresh air soothes my still swirling thoughts. When we arrive at my bedroom door, River stops and turns to me.

"Thank you, Ava. For listening... for giving me a chance to explain."

I smile. Inside my chest, my heart is jumping like a kangaroo. Once again, I feel like hiding behind my mane, but just as I lower my head, River raises it with the tip of his index finger.

"Don't hide. You're beautiful."

"Thank you," I dare say.

He makes a gesture, as if to say something more, then changes his mind.

"Good night, Ava. If you need anything, you know where to find me."

"Good night, River," I say softly, watching him walk away, before returning to my room.

Once inside, I find Julia sitting on her bed, book in hand. She looks up at me, and I can see she's dying of curiosity.

"How did it go?"

I sigh, settling down next to her.

"Better than I could have imagined. He's apologized, Julia. He's acknowledged his mistakes, and he wants to help set the record straight."

Julia puts down her book, her attention focused entirely on me.

"Wow, I wasn't expecting that. That's good news, isn't it?"

"Yes, it's good news. He even said he was going to talk to the team and Bethany, explain that it was his fault, not mine."

As I tell him all this, my heart feels lighter.

"That's brave of him. What about Peter? Did he mention it?" she asks, one eyebrow raised. "Because... I got the impression he was a bit jealous."

I laugh lightly.

"Yes, he mentioned it. He owes him a beer for standing up for me. River realized he cared about me, thanks to Peter. But I clarified the situation with him and... I told him I wouldn't be going out with Peter."

"So, you and River...?"

"Still not official, but I have the impression that it reassured him."

"It's pretty amazing, Ava. It really is."

A warm smile lights up her face.

"I'm so happy for you. It must be a relief, right?" she asks.

"More than you can imagine. I feel... light, like a huge weight has been lifted from my shoulders. But I'm also a little nervous about what's to come. The conversation with the team, with Bethany..."

"I'll be fine, okay? Just try not to think about it right now. At least River believes you, and that's what counts. Because... he's the one you love, isn't he?"

I suddenly stiffen.

The word is strong!

"Uh... well..."

"Right?"

"Yes, of course, yes... I... I like him, that's clear."

And I just admitted it out loud, in front of Julia's radiant smile.

"In that case, you'll do me the pleasure of telling him, won't you? The point is not to let him slip through your fingers. Just take the fucking lead!"

"I don't want to sound like I'm putting this off until tomorrow, but... I've had my share of emotions for today."

And if it wasn't me or Peter who damaged the uniforms... then... who?

The next day, I wake up with a lump in my stomach, the anxiety of returning to class and facing the stares and whispers weighing heavily on me. Despite the support of Julia, Peter and now River, the idea of facing all those students who have judged me, believed, or fed the rumors, is terrifying. I feel like I'm going to be the main topic of discussion again, and I don't want that at all.

I drag my feet to the amphitheater. Each step echoes my apprehension. I can't even hear Julia speaking to me. Today's lecture will put me in the spotlight... there are so many other students present! The whole class will be there. I discreetly take a seat at the back of the room, hoping to go unnoticed, and the professor begins his lecture by diving straight into the topic of the day, but I can't help feeling the stares turning my way, hearing the hushed whispers.

It's unbearable.

My head is already in my hands. At any moment, I'm ready to leave the lecture hall and run away again.

Suddenly, the amphitheater door swings open, drawing everyone's attention. River bursts in, to everyone's surprise, including that of the professor, who stops talking, visibly displeased by the interruption.

"Sir, I'm going to have to ask you to leave immediately," scolds the teacher with authority.

173

"No."

River doesn't seem to mind the reprimand. He strides forward. His gaze sweeps the room until he finds me. Without hesitation, he climbs onto the nearest desk - the teacher's desk.

"Would you mind if I borrowed your desk for a few moments?"

"Uh... I do mind indeed!"

"Sorry, then. I know I'm not allowed to do this," he begins. "But it's important."

His voice carries throughout the amphitheater.

"I owe something to Ava, and to all those who believed or spread rumors about her."

There's total silence, all eyes on him. River takes a deep breath before continuing, and I can't believe what I'm seeing.

"Ava didn't do anything. I'm the one who was careless with the team shirts. She's been wrongly accused, and I'm here to make sure everyone knows it. She deserves an apology, from me and from those who judged her without knowing. You want to understand how the jerseys got ruined, don't you? I'll tell you."

He's really going to do it...

The professor seems about to intervene, but something in River's determined attitude makes him hesitate. The whispers start up again, some of surprise, others of admiration for his courage in revealing himself.

"Peter's even been accused. Sorry, Pete! That was the official version, because this guy, who everyone pushes around like a nobody, is really a nice guy. We thought he'd be the ideal culprit because, well... the guy never says anything. He's almost the type to apologize when he takes a punch. Inevitably, it was a no-brainer. Then it was Ava. Supposedly out of jealousy. The truth is, neither of them is responsible. I'm the one who was negligent in leaving the locker-room door open. And

174

why, I ask you?"

River casts an amused glance in the professor's direction. He has all the mischief in the world in his eyes.

"Because I was banging a classmate in the showers after dumping Bethany."

This time, laughter fills the room, as the teacher turns red and piles up the reasons for River's expulsion and detention.

"I... I'm sorry, Ava. For all the pain, this has caused you. And I'm willing to do whatever it takes to make it right," he concludes. "I needed to say it because you're a great girl and I'm sick of you not seeing it. Maybe that's the worst of it. You're special and you act like you're just like everyone else. The truth is, you're the most interesting, kind and understanding person I've ever met. And, let's face it, you're hot too."

"Sir, have you finished?!" the teacher is impatient.

"I'm declaring my love right now, sir."

"You'll have to declare it elsewhere!"

"No way! So, Ava, I admit I didn't do so well with you, but how about giving it a shot anyway?"

I don't know what to say, and once again, all eyes turn to me. I feel as if I'm on one of the giant screens that film the crowd of spectators during the games.

Frantically, I nod, bringing my hands to my mouth.

He's nuts. Completely nuts.

And my movements are enough to make him smile.

He jumps off the desk, then runs in my direction to kiss me in front of everyone with indescribable passion. Having done so, he greets the professor with a wave of his hand.

"I won't trouble you any further, Mr. Filtzkroft, but... the answer is protactinium," he says, pointing to the blackboard. "At least, I think so. I only glanced at it for a few seconds!"

Without another word, he leaves the room, blowing me a kiss with his hand.

Damn it!

I stand there transfixed, my hands still in front of my mouth, completely overwhelmed by what has just happened. All around me, the students murmur again, some shocked, others amused by the spectacle they've just witnessed. Professor Filtzkroft, for his part, seems totally overwhelmed by the events. He shakes his head in disapproval before trying to resume his lecture, as if nothing had happened.

"Well, er... he... he was right, though. It was the protactinium. But you don't have to get up on my desk to tell me that."

The students laugh and life seems to return to normal.

But for me, nothing will ever be the same again. River has changed the game, not only by coming to my defense so publicly and unexpectedly, but also by declaring his feelings in front of everyone. His bold gesture swept away my last uncertainties and filled my heart with an unprecedented warmth.

After class, I rush out of the amphitheater to get some air, still reeling from this moment of intimacy shared in front of so many witnesses. I feel my phone vibrate in my pocket, but I ignore it, my mind still fully occupied by River and his kiss.

"You're hot." His words echo in my head, and it makes me smile in spite of myself. River saw in me what I was struggling to recognize, and he chose the most unlikely time and way to make me understand it.

Julia grabs my arm as soon as I step outside, a broad smile on her face.

"So, how do you feel after that? It was... spectacular!"

I laugh, still a little dizzy.

"I don't know... Happy, I guess. And completely stunned. He's... incredible."

"You said it! And now?" she asks, curious.

Now I know things will never be the same. River not only

defended my honor, but also opened his heart, changing our relationship forever.

"Now I guess we'll see where it all goes. One thing's for sure, I'm willing to give it a shot."

I don't have time to fully savor the moment when my phone vibrates again. This time, I decide to check, curious as I am to know who is trying to reach me in such a whirlwind of emotions. My heart sinks as I see a notification of a direct message on social networks. It's from Bethany.

Her message is brief, but full of meaning:

★ **Bethany:** *Chemistry room. 2 p.m. Alone.*

I can feel the anxiety soaring. Why would Bethany want to see me now, after all that's happened? Despite my misgivings, part of me knows I have to go, if only to confront what's left of this story and hopefully put an end to all this tension.

"What is it?" asks Julia.

It's 1:50 p.m.

"Uh... nothing. I gotta go."

"You're going to see River, aren't you? Naughty!"

"Yes, that's it."

I make my way to the chemistry room with an apprehension I can't quite shake. Each step echoes through the deserted corridor, amplifying the tension inside me. I push open the door to the chemistry room and find Bethany, arms crossed, a furious expression painted on her face.

"So, you came," she spits without preamble.

"Yes, Bethany. You wanted to talk to me, right?"

I try to keep my voice neutral, despite the ball of anxiety growing in my stomach.

"Talk? Oh, I'll do more than talk. You really think you can get away with this? After all the trouble you've caused?"

177

Her voice is acid, every word as sharp as a stab.

I take a deep breath, trying to stay calm.

"Bethany, I didn't cause any harm. The stories about the jerseys..."

"Shut up about your jerseys!" she interrupts me abruptly. "That's not why I'm angry. It's about River. You've turned his head with your innocent airs and now look! He's making public statements, ruining his reputation for you!"

I'm baffled by the intensity of her anger as I realize that her problem with me goes far beyond jerseys or rumors.

"Bethany, River and I are..."

"What?" she challenges me with her eyes. "Do you think you've won? You think it's all over now that he's defended you to everyone? Well, you're wrong. River will never truly be yours. And I'm going to make sure everyone knows what kind of person you really are."

Her threat is clear, and I feel my courage waver.

"Bethany, I don't want to be your enemy. I just..."

"Too late for that, sweetie. You'll see how it feels when you play with me."

I have a feeling it's going to end badly again.

"What are you going to do?"

"Oh, I have plenty of ideas on how to make you look bitchy. How do you figure? There's no shortage of imagination."

I swallow hard.

"Taking care of the jerseys was just the tip of the iceberg, I can go much further."

"What... what? It was you?! But..."

I stop, shocked by her revelation. My mind is a blur as I try to make sense of her words. Bethany looks at me with a satisfied smile, as if reveling in my confusion.

"Yes, it was me. Surprising? Not really, when you think about it. Everyone was so busy pointing the finger at you, or even Peter, that they didn't even consider other possibilities," she explains.

Her tone becomes more sinister.

"I'm the one who ripped the shirts, and blaming you was so easy. The truth is, you're just the little geek. I mean, what do you think? That you can pull your weight, one way or another?"

"But why? Why do this?"

My voice is barely audible, overwhelmed by confusion and betrayal.

"Why? Because I was sick of it. Sick of River hanging around you, sick of the attention he was giving you. And I knew it would cause problems between you two. It was so easy, Ava. You were the perfect target," Bethany continues with her cold stare. "Originally, damaging the equipment was just to get back at him for breaking up with me. But then you came along. So, I killed several birds with one stone, and accused you."

I feel anger rising inside me, a rage against the injustice of her jealousy, against the ease with which she manipulated the situation to her advantage. This girl is impossible! If she doesn't get her act together, she'll go on and on and on.

"You don't have the right to play with people's lives like that! You've caused so much harm... for what? Because you were jealous? That's pathetic," I retort, my voice trembling with anger.

Bethany rolls her eyes. Her annoyance is obvious.

"Pathetic or not, it worked. Look at the chaos I've created. And I'm not stopping there. If you thought everything was just going to work out because River stood up for you, you're wrong. I'm going to make sure you regret ever coming between me and him."

I look at her and suddenly realize the extent of her determination to harm me. A shiver runs down my spine.

"You won't get away with this, Bethany. The truth always comes out in the end."

"But by then, how much damage would I have done? How many people will turn their backs on you?"

She sketches a cruel smile and I lower my eyes.

"Think about it, Ava. You're alone in this battle. And blaming you for the jerseys was just the beginning. I can make your life a living hell. You have no idea."

"I can accuse you too," I say.

She bursts out laughing.

"Accuse me? Me?"

She looks cute and naive.

"But who would dare? Who would believe you, the nerd, when I'm the hottest cheerleader on campus? The rules are strict. College is the law of nature: lions go with lions. Fleas like you fornicate with lice. Is that clear? Try to break free from your little condition again and I'll make you pay a hundred-fold. You've no idea of the ingenuity I'm capable of deploying to destroy you."

"You're a bitch."

"A bitch with a nice smile, darling. You and River will pay for this."

As she goes to leave the room, this time it's me who gets in her way.

"Uh... what the hell are you doing?" she spits, glaring at me from head to toe.

"Want to play? Sure. I'll tell you what. I don't even care. You can pick on me all you want."

As I move forward with determination, Bethany steps back, frowning.

"You can threaten me, humiliate me, destroy me, bring me to my knees as much as you like, but don't touch River."

"Are you kidding me?"

"I am absolutely serious."

"And what are you going to do?"

"Kick your ass," I say calmly.

I feel a new energy flowing through me and I can hardly recognize myself. But the idea of her hurting River drives me crazy.

"OK, I think you forgot one detail... several in fact... you're short, not very athletic and rather unfit, so..."

Before she can continue, I jostle her, and she crashes into the desk behind her.

"But very pissed off. So, you'd better fuck off. Because two can play at that game. Ruin my reputation if you want, but don't touch River's. And when it comes to gambling, believe me, I know my stuff."

Bethany gives me a haughty, surprised look, then leaves the room, leaving me alone with my tormented thoughts. Bethany's threat weighs heavily on me, the reality of her warning chilling my blood. I know I must act, and quickly, before she puts her plans into action.

"I'm telling you you're going to be perfect," Julia says.

"I'm not sure..."

"Your dress is to die for. And Mark's work on it is incredible. He really has his touch, hasn't he?" she continues.

Shortly after my altercation with Bethany, I received a message. THE message. It was River and he told me that to celebrate his team's victory at the game, they were throwing a big party. The campus director agreed, and apparently, it's going to be the party of the century. Almost everyone is invited. So, for the occasion, I decided to take matters into my own hands and sew myself a dress, with the help of all the members of the sewing club. But now, all of a sudden, I'm not so sure...

I still haven't managed to talk to my friends about Bethany's confessions about the hockey team jerseys. Maybe it's because I don't want to bring dishonor on her, as she did with me... Maybe it's because I want to find a favorable outcome to this situation without going through the direct accusation. I don't really know why I didn't say anything, but for now, I'm still giving myself the chance to use this information.

If she pushes me too far, I'll act.

But as she so rightly pointed out, I'm also a little afraid that people will say I'm trying to keep her away from River for good by ratting her out. And it makes me sick to think that anyone would believe I could use the same disgusting ploys she did.

So there, I didn't say anything.

I glance at my phone: 6:53p.m. Shit, shit, shit... River is going to pick me up from the bedroom at 7p.m. I'm stressing to death!

"I feel like you're breaking down! Come on, relax, it'll be fine, okay?"

I stand in front of the mirror, examining the dress I created with the precious help of my friends. It's a deep, almost mystical blue, with touches of light created by silver threads subtly integrated into the fabric. The dress hugs my curves perfectly, floating slightly above the knee. A perfect balance of elegance and simplicity. Mark added his personal touch to the back, a discreet but eye-catching detail that makes the piece unique. It's a work of art, and yet I can't help doubting it.

My heart is pounding. The events of the last few days, the altercation with Bethany, and now this invitation from River... everything mixes together in my head creating a whirlwind of emotions. Fear, excitement, anticipation, and above all, uncertainty. If Bethany is going to make a move at some point, it's going to be tonight.

"You look beautiful, Ava. Really," insists Julia.

I look at her in the mirror, trying to see what she sees.

"You think so?"

I can't help doubting. Nervousness tightens my chest.

"Absolutely. River won't believe his eyes," she smiles, trying to reassure me.

I smile weakly in return. My gaze is caught by my reflection. Julia is right, the dress is beautiful, and I worked hard on it. It's a manifestation of who I am, my passion for sewing, and my desire to stand tall despite challenges. It's an armor as much as a statement.

"Okay," I let out, taking a deep breath to try and calm my racing heart. Let's go.

"You're going to be perfect."

Just a few more minutes and he'll be here. My stomach hurts.

I hear a message notification on my computer and head for the device.

"Hey! Where are you going? Tonight's not geek night, okay? It can wait!"

"Just a second."

It's Maeline. She sends me a message to wish me luck.

★ **Maeline466:** *Come on, gorgeous. You're going to tear it up. If I see you online before midnight, I swear I'll blow you away!*

I type a 'I promise' in reply, followed by a smiley face.

She deserves my interest in this evening. She's been very supportive lately.

When River knocks on the door, my stomach loops. Julia gives me one last encouraging smile before opening the door. River is there, more handsome than ever, and his eyes light up when he sees me.

"Wow, Ava, you're... incredible," he says, clearly speechless.

I blush, lowering my eyes for a moment before raising them to meet his gaze.

"Thank you, you look very elegant too. I love the suit."

The drive to the party venue is a mixture of comfortable silence and light conversation. When we arrive, the party is already in full swing, but I feel ready. Ready to face the stares, the whispers, even Bethany if necessary. This dress, this party, is my moment to shine, to show everyone that I'm not who they think I am.

Behind this door stand almost every student on campus, and it's the moment of truth. River offers me his arm, so that we can walk together.

As I cling to him, I feel a wave of courage wash over me. We push open the door together, and immediately all eyes turn to us. There's silence for a moment, as if the whole party is holding its breath to welcome us. Then, almost immediately, conversation resumes, but I can feel the admiring glances, the whispers that are intended to be discreet, but which reach me, nonetheless. This time, the eyes are not full of judgment. Quite the opposite, in fact. What a... strange feeling!

"Have you seen Ava? She's gorgeous!"

"It's true, she and River make a great couple."

Compliments pour in from all sides, and I gradually feel the anxiety leave me, replaced by a strange sense of pride. The dress, my armor, seems to have won over the hearts of the skeptics. At this moment, surrounded by light and music, at River's side, I feel invincible.

But as we make our way through the crowd, my eyes meet Bethany's. She's there, leaning against a wall, a glass in her hand, with her two friends. Her expression is hard to read. Her gaze betrays neither the expected anger nor jealousy, but rather a kind of defiance, as if she were advising me to enjoy my fleeting victory. It's as if she's planning to pull off the coup of a lifetime.

No, it's more than that. Because I see a smile.

I squeeze River's arm lightly, seeking comfort in his presence. He looks at me, one eyebrow raised, as if silently questioning me. I offer him a reassuring smile.

I don't want to spoil this moment with unfounded concerns.

Still, I'm sorry I didn't come with Julia. I can see her coming a little further along, with the other members of the sewing club. But now that I'm River's girlfriend, I feel I'm not entitled to the same attention as before. It's like everything has become easier for me.

We head over to the hockey team and right away I congratulate each of the players on their impressive victory in the game.

"Well done, guys. You... you were great," I say.

One by one, they slap my hand.

"It's all thanks to River," retorts one. "He was great because he knew his favorite cheerleader was in the stands."

Point to the heart. They're talking about Bethany.

They laugh, and one of them resumes:

"River played for you, you know, that day."

My eyes widen in surprise.

"Stop being stupid for a moment," says River, almost embarrassed by his teammates' admission. "You've been good, but we're not going to relax."

The atmosphere is one of warm camaraderie. River is at ease among them. His role as undisputed leader is evident even in these relaxed moments. But as the hugs and laughter flow, I notice Peter, a little way back, his usual shy smile on his lips.

"I'll be back in a moment," I apologize to River.

He nods in agreement, and I head for Peter.

"Hey, Peter, I just wanted to say... Thank you. Thanks for everything you've done," I begin. "I know you talked to River and risked getting your ass kicked, as well as wanting to kick River! It's... it's too touching."

I feel charged with sincere gratitude.

Peter looks at me, surprised at first, then a smile lights up his face.

"It was the least I could do, Ava. I'm just glad it all worked out for you. I can't stand injustice like this. I've been through too much not to rebel when I see it coming."

I laugh softly, aware that without his intervention, the situation could have been much worse.

"No, really, Peter. You were incredible. You risked a lot to defend me. I won't forget that. People who... have already suffered a lot of injustice... we stick together."

He blushes slightly, looking away before returning his gaze to me.

"Ava, it's okay. You're my friend now, and that means a lot to me."

I'm moved by his words and realize how lucky I am to have a friend like Peter. Even though he hardly knows me.

"Thank you so much. And know that I'll always be here for you too."

As I return to River, I feel Bethany's gaze following me, but I choose to ignore it. For now, I just want to enjoy the evening, surrounded by people who support and appreciate me for who I am. But deep down, I know that confrontation with Bethany is inevitable.

Julia rushes over to me with the others from the sewing club.

"Wow, this party is really great! It's the first one I've attended!"

"What about your evenings out of the bedroom?"

"You know very well it was for sewing or watching Netflix, so don't act surprised."

Mark approaches us with a smile on his face:

"Damn, that dress looks great on you!"

"It's all thanks to you."

"Oh, please, you've sewn the rest. Let's just say it's a group effort!"

As I laugh with Julia and the other members of the sewing club, sharing anecdotes and memories of our 'wild' sewing evenings, I sense a presence approaching me. I turn just in time to see Bethany, a glass of dark liquid in her hand, a falsely friendly smile plastered on her face.

"Ava, what a surprise to see you here," she exclaims, as if we haven't seen each other until now.

Her voice is full of false enthusiasm. I don't like this at all. It's a twisted plan, or I don't know anything about vicious cheerleading.

Before I can respond, her arm swings awkwardly, or perhaps too precisely, and the contents of her glass spill onto my dress. A dark stain quickly spreads across the deep blue fabric.

"Oh, I'm so sorry!" she says.

But the tone of her voice and the sparkle in her eyes say otherwise.

I stand there transfixed, surprise and indignation preventing me from finding the words. Julia and the other club members exchange shocked glances, ready to intervene, but I raise a hand to stop them.

"It's all right, Bethany. It was just an accident, wasn't it?"

My voice is calm, but my eyes meet hers and I try to convey all the contempt I feel for her petty gesture.

"Of course. What else? Ho, I see you've brought your band of losers with you," she pretends to be surprised, looking at my friends.

"I've already told you that if you mess with River, I'll destroy you. It's the same for my friends..." I say, menacingly.

"Ah, yes, and what exactly are you going to do?"

I can feel an arena forming around us. Oh, no... this time Bethany has an audience, so she won't give up.

"Stop it."

"No, come on! You're the one who said you were going to beat the shit out of me. So, what are you waiting for?" she retorts, as if I'm the bully, when she's clearly the one who's attacking me.

What's she trying to do? Make me out to be the feisty one?

I see she's pulling something out of her purse.

189

Is that... a brass knuckle?!

"My brother lent me this, see? You'll love it!"

Damn, this time I'm really going to lose my teeth if I go on!

Bethany stretches a petty smile and slips the object to her fingers before I can intervene. There, so close together, no one can see what she's up to.

"We can take this outside right now, geek. What do you think? If you back out, people will still call you a chicken... No guts, no guts..."

She's after me. But I try not to walk into her trap.

"I don't need to confront you outside on the campus lawn to know you're losing it Bethany."

"Really? Am I the one who's provoking you? Who keeps telling me she's gonna kick my ass, huh?"

She turns to look at the spectators, trying to take them to task.

"You heard her, didn't you? She keeps threatening me! It's getting downright creepy! And all this for what? Because I was with River before her! But if I left him, there must be a reason."

She makes a little pout, and I sense that her audience is hanging on her every word, waiting for some juicy revelation.

What the hell is she playing at? Now she wants to go after River's reputation? Was this her plan?

Basically, either I follow her outside and lose my teeth, as well as being accused of jumping down her throat. Or I stand there and listen to her patiently pick apart my boyfriend with lies. I can't even tell her that she's the one who hurt the hockey team, because at this point, you'd be able to tell that I'm just trying to spite her!

Trapped.

The crowd around us is getting restless, and I can see River approaching from the corner of my eye, eyebrows furrowed. On his heels, the members of the hockey team.

It's going to get out of hand...

"Stop it, Bethany," exclaims a voice behind her.

I look up, surprised, coming across one of the university cheerleaders.

"What's the matter with you? Are you going to defend that bitch?"

"Yeah."

"Are you crazy?"

"Ava, I'm sorry," her friend says.

I frown.

"In all this time, I... I've never really had the courage to take responsibility for myself..."

But what is she telling me? Who is this girl?

"It's me," she confesses. "I'm Maeline. My real name is Madeline."

The revelation comes as a shock.

Maeline466! My online friend. My game partner.

"I... I tried to warn you about River. I tried to tell you that guys like that were complicated to deal with. And then, afterwards, I wanted to encourage you, but I knew Bethany would give you a hard time. I'm sorry, I didn't have the courage to really assume who I was. I... I chose the cheerleader mask over the real me."

She leaves a few moments of silence, then resumes:

"But it won't happen again. I promise!"

She takes a tentative step towards me, and pulls over to my side. My mouth is half-open and my eyes still wide. I struggle to gather my thoughts and answer anything.

"You had the courage to assume who you were. So have I. In fact, I think we all should," she says. "I know that not everyone is as smooth as they say they are. Come on, admit it: we're all full of little quirks. Things that are a little out of the ordinary. Isn't that what makes us human? Otherwise, we'd just be clones! And even if that's what the university wants, deep down, it weighs on all of us. So, what if, for once, we just assumed we were... just what we are?"

Madeline's declaration, courageous and sincere, seems to suspend time around us. A murmur runs through the crowd, and I see surprised faces, others nodding slowly, as if awakened from a long sleep by her words. Bethany, her brass knuckles still in hand, seems suddenly diminished. Her weapon loses all its power in the face of Madeline's call for authenticity.

"It's... it's true," says a boy shyly from the back of the room. "I'm a programming geek. And I like my life!"

A girl next to him, with strands of colorful hair, adds:

"I'm a cosplay fan. And I've always been afraid to say it here."

Confessions follow one another, each adding to the edifice of sincerity Madeline has begun to build. It's as if an invisible weight has been lifted from everyone's shoulders, allowing them to breathe a little more freely, to stand a little straighter.

"And I'm a fucking science geek," River suddenly confesses. "I'm not just a sportsman. I'm more than that. I'm more than meets the eye."

I turn to my rival and say:

"What about you, show us who you truly are?"

Bethany, now alone in her aggression, puts the knuckle away quickly and awkwardly, almost dropping it, bewildered by the unexpected solidarity forming in front of her. Her gaze shifts from Madeline to me, then to the others, seeking support where there is none.

"I... I..."

Without warning, she decides to flee, draped in shame. I'm not going to chase after her. Too bad for her. I think she needs to think things through.

I approach my not-so-virtual friend. Emotions swirl inside

me. Anger, indignation, but above all, deep gratitude to this girl for choosing this moment to reveal her true identity and take a stand.

"Maeline, I... Thank you. I don't know what to say," I mutter, moved.

She smiles at me, with a vulnerability I'd never seen in her before. I thought she was just a cheerleader. A friend of Bethany's. But masks are cracking tonight.

"I think we both needed this moment. To show who we really are. And you know what? It feels good."

I nod, looking around. The faces are no longer those of mere spectators to a drama, but of real, complex people, with their own stories, their own fears, and now, their own courage.

River approaches me and puts an arm around my shoulders.

"It's incredible what you've done," he says admiringly. "Does your hair really mean you're a lioness?"

"It's not me!"

But I know that deep down, this moment is the result of all the little sparks of courage we've shared. They fueled an even greater fire.

"Come here, warrior."

River gently draws me to the center of the room, where the music has changed to a slower, more intimate piece. He looks at me with a tenderness I've never seen before. It's pure emotion.

"Would you like to dance?" he asks.

His voice is barely more than a whisper amid the hubbub of the party.

I nod, and he gently pulls me towards him. As we begin to dance, I feel enveloped in a bubble, isolated from the rest of the world. Only River and I exist, and the music guides our steps. His hands on my waist reassure me, make me feel safe, while I rest mine on his shoulders, savoring the warmth of his embrace.

The world around us fades away. It gives way to a moment of rare beauty and intimacy. River guides me with confidence, every movement fluid and perfectly synchronized with mine. I lift my eyes to his, to lose myself in his deep gaze, and see the love he bears me. A pure, unpretentious love that asks nothing in return except to be shared.

"Ava, since I've known you, every day with you has been a gift," he whispers.

His voice is full of emotion.

"I don't know what the future holds," he continues, "but I want you to know that I'm here. For you. Always."

My heart beats wildly, overwhelmed by the love I feel for him, a love that has grown and matured through our ordeals.

"River, I... I love you. I'm afraid of what the future holds, but I know that as long as we're together, we can face anything."

The slow dance ends, but we remain entwined, savoring the warmth of our closeness. Around us, the party continues, but for this suspended moment, nothing else matters but his lips, which he presses to mine with infinite tenderness.

"I love you too, Carrot," he concludes, tucking a lock of hair behind my ear.

The evening continues with dancing, laughter and conversation. River and I are inseparable, and I can feel people's gazes gradually changing. Those who used to judge me, who used to spread rumors, now seem to see another version of me, the one River has always seen.

The support of my friends, the courageous revelation of Madeline, and now, this dance with River, have woven together a new reality where I feel not only accepted, but valued.

As the evening progresses, I notice that conversations with

me become more open, warmer. People come up to me, some to apologize for past behavior, others simply to share a pleasant moment. It's strange how a few sincere actions can change the perception of the people around me.

"This party is AWESOME!" says Julia enthusiastically.

"Yes, huh? I've never been happier, I think."

River stays by my side, protective, but also incredibly proud. He never misses an opportunity to compliment me or make me laugh. It's as if, for the first time, I can truly be myself, without fear or reservation.

"So," he says, "we've told everyone we're a big geek, eh"?

"Don't you like it?"

"I do. Very much so."

But even in this bubble of happiness, I can't help but cast occasional glances around, looking for Bethany. She disappeared after her failure, and I can't help wondering if she's up to something else. For the moment, however, I choose not to let this shadow spoil my evening.

"You were really incredible."

"It wasn't much. Someone had to stand up to her reign of terror, didn't they?"

Julia nods.

"You did!"

"I can be brave."

"Other than in games, yes, as far as I can see."

Which reminds me, I'll have to let Madeline know so we can have a good game tomorrow!

As the party draws to a close, River and I slip outside for a moment to get some fresh air. The campus is silent, bathed in the soft light of the moon. We sit on a bench, our hands entwined, and share a moment of calm after the evening's excitement.

"You know, Ava, no matter what the future holds, I want

195

you to remember this night. The strength you've shown, the love we share. You're amazing, and I'm so lucky to have you in my life," he whispers, his gaze locked in mine.

I lean against him.

"Me too, River. You're far from the sports cliché I'd imagined."

"I hope so!" he laughs.

In the silence of the night, under the benevolent gaze of the stars, we share a kiss, a silent promise to remain united in the face of everything.

"Go, go, go! Go for it, River!

It's the last game of the season and I'm screaming my lungs out in the stands with Madeline and Julia.

The tension in the air is palpable, and every spectator holds his or her breath as the puck zigzags across the ice with frenetic energy. River, our star, our pride and joy, is right in the middle of the action. His movements are fluid, almost choreographed.

The score is close, too close for a game of this importance. It's the final of the season, and the stakes go far beyond the simple trophy. It's a matter of pride, of honor, of irrefutable proof of all the hard work, sweat and tears shed throughout the year. But it's also potentially a rib and a pro career for River. His father is here too, and I know the pressure is on for him.

Coach Harrison isn't far from me. He has his arms crossed and is watching the show with a certain sternness.

"They're playing well. What do you think?"

"Mmh," he retorts in his usual deep voice.

"You... you don't look convinced?"

"I care about River. He carries the whole team. He doesn't know it, but a scout is among the spectators. I didn't want to tell him because I didn't want him to feel pressured. But if he screws up, it's all over."

Suddenly, I'm the nervous one!

I can feel my heart racing at the thought. The pressure on

197

River's shoulders is not just to win this game, but it could determine his entire future. And now, with the revelation of Coach Harrison, that pressure seems to be mounting and becoming almost palpable. I look around, trying to identify this mystery scout among the crowd, but all the faces melt into a sea of anticipation and excitement.

Holy shit!

"He's going to win," I murmur, more to reassure myself than to answer the coach.

Harrison glances at me. There's a mixture of skepticism and hope in his eyes.

"He'd better. He's got the talent, that's for sure. He's just got to keep his cool. But you've had a positive impact on him."

I turn my attention back to the game, searching for River with my eyes. There, in the midst of the commotion, he moves with a confidence that masks any trace of nervousness. Maybe the coach is right. It was better that he didn't know.

The puck glides across the ice, and River intercepts it with remarkable precision. He dodges one opponent, then a second, his speed and dexterity highlighting his natural talent. The crowd's cheers rise to a crescendo, a powerful murmur of support that seems to push him forward.

Come on, you can do it!

The moment is critical. I hold my breath, as do the rest of the spectators, as River fires his shot. Silence falls over the arena, a suspended moment when time seems to stand still.

Then, with incredible strength and precision, he throws the puck. The trajectory is perfect, the goalkeeper dives, but it's too late. The puck crosses the goal line, and a roar of joy explodes around me. River has scored, changing the course of the game in our favor.

The joy is indescribable, a wave of emotion sweeps through the stands. I jump up shouting River's name and share this moment of euphoria with Madeline, Julia and all the other fans. It's good! It's so good!

Coach Harrison lets out a sigh of relief and sketches what looks like a smile.

"That's our boy," he exclaims with undisguised pride.

He even lets out a burst of joy, discreetly shaking his fist. For a cold guy like him, this must be quite exceptional!

The rest of the game was a hard-fought battle, but River's goal gave the team a new energy. When the final buzzer sounds, we're leading by a point. It's victory, a bittersweet victory filled with relief, pride and hope for the future.

At my side, Madeline and Julia are just as committed, their voices mingling with mine to create a cacophony of encouragement. We jump up and down. Come on, he's got to stop making us wait and let them win!

On the pitch, River captures our energy. He glances towards the stands for a brief moment, enough to catch my eye. When his eyes meet mine, I see that he's smiling, and my heart swells with indescribable joy.

The clock ticks down to the final seconds, and the intensity rises a notch. River dodges opponent after opponent with astonishing precision. The crowd holds its breath, time suspended in his movements. Then, in a spectacular burst, he takes off for the final shot.

The silence is deafening, every heartbeat echoing in anticipation of the result. The puck traces a perfect parabola in the air before crossing the goal line with a crisp thud. The buzzer sounds, sealing the fate of the match.

It's victory. An explosion of joy erupts in the stands, a wave of euphoric energy sweeping over everything in its path. Madeline, Julia and I rush out onto the pitch to join River and his team in unbridled celebration. Cheers, applause and shouts of victory fill the air. The atmosphere is electric.

River is overwhelmed by his teammates. They lift him in triumph. His smile eclipses even the brilliance of the trophy they hold up proudly. I make my way through the crowd to him, and our eyes meet again.

"You did it, River! You're incredible!" I exclaim, unable to contain my pride.

"That last goal was for you, sweetheart," he says, kissing me.

"When you've finished smooching your girlfriend, River... Someone wants to see you!" exclaims the coach.

River raises an eyebrow in surprise.

"Who?"

"Follow me."

"Okay, if Ava can come."

Harrison rolls his eyes, but nods.

The coach then leads River and me through the crowd of fans and players, all basking in the euphoria of triumph. He leads us to a quieter part of the stadium, where a man stands aside. He seems to be observing the scene with professional interest. His demeanor exudes a certain self-confidence, that of a person accustomed to spotting talent where it's found.

Oh, my God, it's him!

The man steps towards us as soon as he sees us approach. His gaze is fixed on River, while an appreciative smile stretches his lips.

"River, congratulations on the game. I'm Marc Anderson, scout for the Ranger Beasts. I've been following your performances all season, and what I saw tonight confirms what I already thought."

River exchanges a surprised look with me, then turns to the man, a mixture of nervousness and excitement in his eyes.

"Thank you, sir. I'm honored."

"The honor is mine. You have a natural talent, determination and vision for the game that are rare at this age. We're looking for promising young talent to join our team, and I think you have the potential to be part of this adventure. Even if your university isn't in one of the NCAA's top divisions[7] , I still want to sign you for the NHL[8] .

River's expression is a mixture of disbelief and joy. His eyes shine with a new gleam. He turns briefly to me and a triumphant smile lights up his face, before returning to the man.

"I... I don't know what to say. It's like a dream come true."

Marc Anderson nods.

"Take some time to think, River. We want you to come to an evaluation session with some of our coaches and players. It's an opportunity to see how you fit in with the team, and for us to show you what we can offer you."

"Yes, of course! I'd be delighted to take part."

I feel a wave of pride wash over me. River, with his talent and passion, has caught the eye of a professional recruiter. This is a pivotal moment, not just in his career, but in his life. His dream of playing hockey at a professional level is within reach. His father will be thrilled!

"Thank you very much. I'll give it my best shot," he promises.

Marc Anderson smiles, satisfied.

"That's all we ask. We'll be in touch with you in the next few days to organize everything. Enjoy your victory tonight, you've earned it."

As the man walks away, River turns to me. His eyes sparkle with excitement.

"Can you believe it, Ava? This could change everything."

---

7 National Collegiate Athletic Association: governing body for college and university athletic programs in the United States. Teams are divided into three divisions (I, II and III) based on the size of the school and the size of the athletic scholarships awarded.

8 National Hockey League: North America's leading professional ice hockey league considered the best in the world.

I take his hand.

"I'm so proud of you, River. You've worked so hard for this. This is your moment."

Naturally, River shares the news with his teammates, and the excitement is palpable. They gather around him. The congratulations come from all sides. Each player expresses his joy and pride at their captain's achievement. I expected there to be some jealousy, but on the contrary.

"Can you imagine, Nashville?" says one of them, a dazzling smile on his lips. "It's incredible, man!"

River nods, a shy but radiant smile on his face.

"Yeah, it's a little far, but it's an incredible opportunity. I promise we'll always see each other. You're not getting rid of me that easily!"

They exchange laughs and friendly pats, but in the midst of this celebration, I feel a twinge of regret. The thought of River moving far away, to Nashville, begins to settle in my mind, sowing seeds of anxiety and nostalgia for moments we haven't yet experienced.

I look at River, surrounded by his friends, radiating happiness and excitement for the future. My heart sinks at the thought of him leaving, of knowing he's hundreds of miles away. This sudden reality hits me with unexpected force. Up until now, our future seemed like a blank canvas we could paint together, but now a large part of it will take place in a place I don't know, far away from me.

"Ava, are you coming?"

River's voice draws me out of my thoughts. He's noticed my silence and my distant gaze. I offer him a smile, trying to mask the hurricane of emotions that overwhelms me.

"Yes, of course. I'm here."

I approach him, and he puts an arm around my shoulders. His closeness comforts me, yet the weight of the inevitable separation seems heavier than ever.

"It's a new chapter for you, River. I'm really happy," I say. My voice betrays a hint of melancholy.

"And you're part of it, Ava. Whatever happens, we'll make it work. OK?"

His eyes seek mine.

He wants to reassure me.

"How?"

"I don't know yet. But I don't want to go to Nashville without you."

"Don't talk nonsense. We're talking about your future here! You can't sacrifice everything. Not like this, River."

"But... I'm ready. You know I want to be an athlete and a scientist. Anyway, it hasn't happened yet. And if it's going to happen, it's going to happen next fall."

I remain silent.

"What if... what if you found something in Nashville? Hmm? I don't want to be away from you, Ava," he says.

I look up, astonished by so much attachment.

"You... you think so? But... what about school? What about everything else?"

"As long as it's just the two of us, I'm fine with it. If you don't come, I won't hesitate to stay. I don't want to impose anything on you."

With a heavy heart, I stare at River, amazed at the depth of his commitment to our relationship. The idea that he would consider giving up such an opportunity for me makes me realize the significance of his proposal. His words weigh heavily in the air between us. I can't accept it. It's too much.

"River, I..." I begin, searching my words carefully. "I don't want to be the one you give up your dreams for. You have this incredible chance, and I'd be selfish to ask you to stay."

He pulls me a little closer to him, as if to reassure me with his embrace.

"Ava, I'm not giving up on my dreams if I'm with you. And you're not asking me to. I've made up my mind. Yes, playing hockey at a professional level is a dream, but there are other ways to be happy, other dreams to pursue. And then, who knows? Maybe there are opportunities for you in Nashville too? Universities, internships..."

I'm lulled by his optimism, but I'm still worried. River has always had this ability to see the bright side of things, to imagine solutions where I could only see problems. It's one of the many reasons why I love him so much, after all. He's not just a jock. Far from it.

"We could at least explore the options," he suggests gently. "See what Nashville has to offer for both of us. It's not as if we have to decide now. We have time to think, to plan."

I nod, touched by his determination to find a solution that suits us both.

"Okay," I finally say, a faint smile on my lips. "We'll explore the options. Together."

He returns my smile. His eyes shine with a mixture of hope and love.

"Together," he repeats.

And in his voice, I find the strength to believe that we could indeed face this change, together.

The evening continues in a festive mood, but part of me remains concerned about our future. The prospect of moving to Nashville, of starting a new life far from everything we know is both exciting and terrifying. But knowing that River is by my side, ready to face these uncertainties with me, makes it all a little less daunting.

When I walk through the bedroom door, I find Julia and my little world, which has been turned upside down lately.

"How does it feel? You're dating a real star now! You two

disappeared earlier today. Were you celebrating in your own way?"

I laugh at Julia's remark. In fact, I would have liked to, but no, it wasn't the case.

"Star, maybe, but it's still the same River," I retort as I sit on my bed, staring into space.

I think of all that lies ahead.

Julia sits down next to me. Her expression becomes more serious.

"What's wrong?"

"River was offered the chance to play professionally."

Julia raises her eyebrows. I can see the genuine happiness on her face.

"Isn't it great?"

"Yes. Except... it's in Nashville..."

"Oh, I see, and... this Nashville thing... does it scare you?"

I sigh. It's hard to ignore the truth of my feelings.

"A little, yes. It's a big change. But River suggested we explore the options together. See what Nashville has to offer for both of us."

Julia nods.

"It's a great adventure, honey. And you know, Nashville isn't just about country music and barbecues. There are universities, programs of study that might interest you. Who knows, maybe you'll find your calling, just as River seems to have found his."

Her optimism is contagious, and I can't help but smile at the thought. It would be great, for sure... but I'll miss everything about this place. Whether it's the campus or... her. Not to mention the sewing club!

"You're right. Maybe this is a chance to start something new. To discover myself, away from everything I know. But... you're here and so are the others. I don't want to be away from you."

Julia gives me a friendly tap on the shoulder.

"Stop your nonsense. As if we were going to disappear! And who knows, maybe Nashville will be the start of something big for you too. This is an opportunity to grow, to change, together."

"Together," I repeat, as if the words are echoing in my head. She smiles and gets out of bed.

"So, when do we start looking for info on Nashville? Universities, jobs, life there... We've got work to do, right?"

I laugh. Her determination gives me a much-needed boost.

"Tomorrow. Let's get started tomorrow."

I don't even feel like playing on the computer right now. I slide into bed and keep my gaze fixed on the ceiling.

I don't know what the future holds, but one thing's for sure: I'm in love.

16

It's the end of the year and we've got our work cut out for us. But I've earned the respect and support of all my club partners. Our little group has grown to include new members, each more motivated than the last. And... for the first time, I'm in charge of proposing designs. We're going to finalize them today.

I've gathered the whole club in our premises - where we're starting to feel a bit cramped - but all hands are welcome. We're going to need some elbow grease, and for the occasion, River has even taken the trouble to come along, too. He's waiting patiently for my instructions - just like everyone else.

And I'm clearing my throat, ready to present my creations:

"Hello everyone, and thank you for being here," I begin, feeling a slight nervousness vibrate through me. "Today is a big day for our sewing club. Not only because we're all together to work on a common project, but also because we're going to bring to life creations that I hope will reflect our passion and dedication to the art of sewing."

Julia nods and I realize I'm doing better than the first time: when I took over the club.

I signal to River, who brings me a box containing sketches and drawings of our future projects. I distribute the sketches among the members, allowing them to discover the ideas we'll be working on.

"Here are the designs I've imagined for our next collection. Each piece has been designed to highlight not only our technical skills, but also our ability to innovate and create unique garments that reflect who we are. Mark, I'm thinking of you right now."

He winks at me.

I present the first design: an elegant dress with handmade embroidery details, blending tradition and modernity. Then I move on to a unisex jacket with clean lines, designed to be both functional and stylish.

"For each piece, I thought about how we could incorporate elements that are dear to us, such as durability, originality and personalization. I want our collection to reflect our community: diverse, creative and committed."

I look around for reactions. Faces are focused, some members are nodding in approval, and I can see excitement in the eyes of a few.

"But to make it happen, I need you. Your ideas, your talent and your commitment. Today, we're going to form small teams, each responsible for one aspect of the project. Whether it's design, fabric selection, sewing or finishing, each task is crucial to the success of our collection. I'm counting on each and every one of you!"

I pause and inhale deeply to calm my nerves, under Julia's guidance as she gestures with her hands.

"And I'm so happy that River is here with us today. He may not be into sewing, but his support shows that our passion can bring people together far beyond our small circle."

My boyfriend gives me an encouraging smile, and I feel a wave of pride wash over me. This is an important moment for me. For all of us.

"So, are you up for the challenge? Working together to make this collection a reality?"

The enthusiastic responses fill the room, and I can feel the positive energy flowing between us. Today, we're not just a sewing club. We're a team, a family, and as River is the captain of the hockey team, I feel like the captain of this team too.

"Perfect! Let's distribute the tasks and get started. We've got work to do, but I know we can do it."

And with those words, the sewing club gets moving, while I oversee operations.

The work is studious but imbued with a contagious passion. Each member of the club tackles his or her task with total dedication. Their skillful hands bring the fabrics to life. Sewing machines hum, scissors glide over fabric, and pins hold it all together as designs take shape. And, before my astonished eyes, I see simple ideas transformed into tangible creations.

The concentration is palpable, but the atmosphere remains light, buoyed by laughter and encouraging exchanges. Tips and tricks are shared at every turn, and each member brings his or her own unique expertise to the joint project and to each other. River, even if he's not a seamstress, finds his place helping to move materials, hold fabrics, and offer encouragement.

As the hours go by, however, fatigue begins to set in. Inevitably, shoulders slump slightly, and eyes grow tired. That's when I decide it's time to boost morale - like a real captain!

"Take a break, everyone!" I announce.

Heads perk up, curious, as I bring out cold drinks and an assortment of cakes I'd prepared in advance. Everyone approaches with a grateful smile on their lips, happy for a well-deserved break.

"You've all worked incredibly hard today," I say, handing out the refreshments. "It's important to take a moment to relax and recharge. We've accomplished a lot! Especially you, Madeline."

She gives me a look full of benevolence.

"Oh, it's nothing..."

"Not at all, not at all. You outdid yourself. And you dared to come here. With the geeks," Mark adds with a smile.

Conversations start up again, more animated, as everyone enjoys the break. Laughter erupts and the atmosphere warms up with drinks and sweet treats.

River slides in beside me, giving me a hug.

"You're incredible, you know?" he whispers in my ear. "You have a gift for bringing people together and bringing out the best in them. I think we might be cut from the same cloth after all?"

I snuggle up to him, touched by his words.

"It's because I'm surrounded by the best people. And you're one of them."

"Are you trying to seduce me, Carrot?"

"I'm getting there, aren't I?"

"Let's just say it's not too bad. But... I think you're a good captain. I mean it!"

As the break draws to a close, the energy in the room is renewed. Club members are returning to their work with renewed momentum, motivated by the break and the shared vision of our project. With this close-knit team, I have no doubt that our collection will be a success. I'm sure it will work, and that I'll have some great projects to showcase on my résumé. Because once I've finished my studies, I'll be looking for work in Nashville.

It's at times like these that I realize the importance of community, friendship and shared passion. Together, we're able to overcome fatigue, rise to challenges and create something beautiful. And as I watch our sewing club at work, I can't help but feel incredibly grateful for every person present, for every moment shared. Even Peter puts his heart into his work. In fact, River officially tells him that he's better at sewing than hockey.

"You'd better watch out, Ava," River calls out to me. "Soon, the club won't need you anymore. Peter will replace you single-handedly. He's a real artist!"

And he pats his shoulder vigorously. Ah, it's him all right, my great sportsman who's not as dumb as he looks. And it's partly thanks to him that I now have the confidence to be so much in the limelight. He gave me the strength. I get out of my comfort zone, and he sees beyond appearances. I think it's a fine balance in the end!

"And what exactly are all these extra pieces of fabric for?"

I have a little plan for that...

"Well, I'm glad you asked. I had the idea of... well... offering my creations for sale."

"What? Are you serious?"

"So, you're going for it?" asks Julia. "That's great!"

"I think I can get orders if I do well. But just so we're clear, I'm not asking you to work for me for nothing. No, I'm not. We'll all get credit for it. But now that the club is making money from repairing jerseys, I think we can make a bit of money out of it, don't you?"

Everyone nods in agreement. It's not like we stole it! It's been so hard. It's been such an adventure to get this reward...

"I'm behind you one hundred percent on this," adds Madeline. "I'm sure you'll be a big hit. Your designs are super classy. Am I right?"

River steps in to nod proudly.

"That's for sure. My half-blind tigress has quite an imagination!"

"You're referring to my glasses, aren't you?"

"Of course!"

I raise my head to challenge him gently with my eyes. He cracks me up, the idiot. But, more important than all that, he's taught me to have greater self-confidence, because now: I don't hide anymore. At all.

EPILOGUE

Life in Nashville is a lot sweeter than I imagined. Since River turned pro, he's been earning a real salary, which has enabled us to get an apartment together.

It's a big step for us, but the transition has been surprisingly smooth. Maybe because, despite the changes, some things remain the same. Like my online game nights with Julia, Peter, and Madeline. It's become our little ritual, a way of staying connected despite the distance that separates us.

Julia, who had never really played before, dived headfirst into this universe so as not to feel left out. She started with simple games, but under Peter's patient guidance and Madeline's encouragement, she quickly became a fully-fledged member of our team. Our play sessions have become moments of pure pleasure – even though we sometimes annoy River when he's trying to sleep. It's our way of keeping in touch.

"Take it easy, you lot! I'm a beginner!"

"You'll improve," adds Madeline. "Peter's coaching you, isn't he?"

"Hey, all fair and square," replies the interested party.

And I burst out laughing when I hear the gossip of their lives. I understand that Julia and Peter have grown closer, yes: but I didn't know it was that close. At the same time, between the sewing club and video games now, they share a lot in common.

These moments of online gaming have become more than just distractions; they're a constant reminder of the importance of friendship and connection. No matter where life takes us, these bonds remain intact, nourished by our shared adventures, virtual or otherwise.

"We're still coming next week, right?" asks Madeline.

"We're waiting for you. River is impatient."

"Him? Seriously?" asks Julia.

"I swear to God. He's looking forward to it. He misses his old life too, you know. Now he's more popular than ever. But... in real life. Not just on social networks or on campus, so...."

"Yeah, I see," says Madeline. "Well, he'll be happy to see we haven't changed a bit."

"Speak for yourself," retorts Julia, "I've really become addicted to these games. I think it's even worse than drugs."

Living in Nashville has also been an opportunity to discover a new community. The sewing club I joined offered me a space to share my passion and meet some extraordinary people. It's fascinating to see how, no matter where you are, you can find people who share the same interests and values. This community has quickly become a second family. It's an indispensable support in the city I now call home. I needed to find myself here. There's the club, a great café nearby and even... a relic of the past: a video game store that actually sells CDs and retrogaming. Crazy enough to mention!

River, for his part, has adapted to his new professional life with the same enthusiasm and determination that characterize him on the ice. His support has been my rock. It helped me navigate through the uncertainties and joys of this new adventure. His ability to see beyond appearances and encourage me to step out of my comfort zone has been a priceless gift. Together, we found a perfect balance, a mix of mutual support, love and ambition. Plus, the apartment isn't bad at all! I can't say we're unhappy. Far from it.

Just then, the door opens with a thud and River enters, looking exhausted but happy after a long training session. Without missing a beat, he makes his way over to me, gently pulls me out of my chair and gives me a kiss that instantly makes me forget the virtual world I'd been immersed in.

"Hello, gorgeous," he murmurs, his breath warm against my ear. "How's the game going?"

I laugh, reluctantly detaching myself to pick up my headset again.

"Guys, River just got home. He says hello."

Over the loudspeakers, I can hear the enthusiastic responses of Julia, Peter and Madeline, each with their own greeting or joke.

"He's going to say hello to your panties," dares Julia.

Then Peter, with his usual sense of humor, issues an invitation that captures my lover's attention.

"Hey, River, feel like joining us for a game? We could use an extra pro on the team."

River bursts out laughing, his eyes sparkling with mischief and amusement.

"Are you sure you want me? I'm in danger of lowering the team's standards."

"No, don't worry!" Madeline replies. "It might be funny to see you trying to follow us."

With a knowing smile, River accepts the invitation and settles down next to me, so that I can guide him through the game. It's a simple moment, but incredibly meaningful.

The evening quickly turns into a series of frenzied games, with laughter and teasing coming from all sides - rather like every other evening, after all. River, despite his initial protests, turns out to be a fierce competitor. I have to be honest: he sucks. Very bad, in fact. But he's determined, and his stub-

215

bornness brings a new dynamic to our virtual team. It's in these moments of shared joy that I realize how rich and full our life in Nashville has become. How, in the end, things haven't changed all that much.

Life here has its challenges, of course, but it's also filled with unexpected moments of happiness, new friendships, and opportunities to explore what it really means to be together. Whether it's through online games, sewing sessions, or simply sharing our daily lives, River and I have found our place together.

As the ring on my finger testifies, my life continues to change, and for once, it's for the better.

I can't wait to tell them all.

Yes, I can't wait!

A week later, our Nashville apartment is busier than ever. It's a special day, not only because the sun is shining brighter than usual, but also because Julia, Peter, and Madeline are on their way to visit us. River and I have planned this visit with barely contained excitement, a secret shared between us.

When they arrive, the hugs are warm, the laughter is hearty, and the atmosphere is filled with palpable joy. We settled into the lounge, cold drinks in hand. Naturally, they were all curious to see what our little home would look like, and they weren't disappointed.

"Well, old chap," says Peter. "Looks like you're not making too bad a living, eh?"

"Oh, you're going to be disappointed, but... it's all thanks to Ava."

I haven't dared talk about it until now, but I'm rather proud, yes...

"What? What are you talking about? Are you keeping secrets from us?"

They have no idea how much.

"I have to say that orders aren't doing too badly, as far as sewing is concerned. I make collectors' items and people snap them up on Vinted."

"No way! Are you kidding me?!"

"I swear to God. It's a daydream!"

"Bravo! So, you're not just a monster killer. You're also an amazing seamstress, I see."

"We already knew that," exclaims Julia. "By the way, what's new in Nashville?" she asks with a mischievous smile on her lips.

River and I exchange a knowing glance, the moment we've been waiting for is finally here.

"We've got something to tell you," begins River.

His hand finds mine.

I can feel my heart racing, the anticipation making butterflies dance in my stomach.

"We're engaged," I reveal, holding up my hand to show them the ring sparkling on my finger.

A moment of silence, then the room explodes in exclamations of surprise and congratulations. Julia leaps to her feet and hugs me with a strength that testifies to her joy.

"Oh, Ava! How wonderful!" she exclaims.

She even has tears of happiness in the corner of her eyes.

Peter and Madeline join her.

"I knew that guy was a keeper," jokes Peter, giving River a friendly pat on the shoulder.

"I'm a captain, actually."

"You're perfect for each other," adds Madeline.

Her smile is as wide as mine.

The conversation then turns to wedding plans. Ideas flow, some extravagant, like dove releases, and other more traditional, like French cuisine. But in the midst of it all, what stands out is the love and unconditional support of our friends.

River pulls me closer, an arm around my hips. His gaze on me is filled with love and promise.

"Looks like we'll have to plan one hell of a party," he whispers in my ear.

"Yeah, and we want something other than a campus party, right, warns Peter. We're talking about a wedding!"

I laugh, leaning against River, his arm still around me. The atmosphere is electric, filled with anticipation and excitement for the future. But in the midst of all this excitement, an inner peace settles over me. I've always known that River was my favorite person on Earth - well, if I'm being honest, I've known it for a few months now, because I used to loathe jocks - but announcing our engagement to our closest friends makes it all the more real, more tangible.

"One thing's for sure, I want everyone to be here," I say. "You've all played such an important role in our lives. It wouldn't be the same without you."

River nods in silent agreement.

"And," he adds, with a wry smile, "we need witnesses for our future online gaming exploits, don't we? And... er... for the wedding too, of course."

The laughter that follows is a mixture of joy and complicity. It's at times like this that I realize how strong a bond we've forged, despite the distance and changes in our lives. Nashville didn't just bring us a new home or opportunities: it offered us a new chapter in our lives, enriched by love, friendship, and now, a shared future. Commitments. Promises.

It's a dream I never imagined I'd have, but now that I'm living it, I can't imagine being anywhere else.

It's a beautiful life, a life full of love, adventure, and now, a promising future. And I'm infinitely grateful for every moment of this journey, eager to see where the road takes us next.

But one thing is certain: as long as we're together, anything is possible.

Our books are also available in e-book. Find our catalog on:
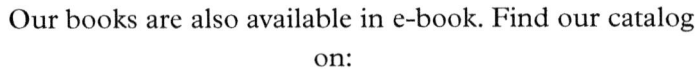
https://cherry-publishing.com/en/

Subscribe to our newsletter and receive a free e-book! You'll also receive the latest updates on all of our upcoming publications!

https://mailchi.mp/b78947827e5e/get-your-free-ebook

Unexpected Partners

Editorial manager: Audrey Puech
Composition and layout: Cherry Publishing
Interior Illustrations: © Shutterstock
Cover design: Keti Matakov
Cover illustration: Keti Matakov

Unexpected Partners

Printed in Great Britain
by Amazon

42010841R00128